First Annual
Conference Proceedings

Microcomputers in K-12 Education

OTHER BOOKS OF INTEREST

S.I. Ahmad and K.T. Fung
Introduction to Computer Design and Implementation

Wayne Amsbury
Structured Basic and Beyond

Pierre Barrette, Editor
Microcomputers in K–12 Education

M. Carberry, H. Khalil, J. Leathrum, and L. Levy
Foundations of Computer Science

Erik L. Dagless and David Aspinall
Introduction to Microcomputers

William Findlay and David Watt
Pascal: An Introduction to Methodical Programming, Second Edition

Rachelle Heller and C. Dianne Martin
Bits 'n Bytes About Computing: A Computer Literacy Primer

Harold Lawson
Understanding Computer Systems

David Levy
Chess and Computers

David Levy and Monroe Newborn
More Chess and Computers: The Microcomputer Revolution and the Challenge Match

Tom Logsdon
Computers and Social Controversy

Ira Pohl and Alan Shaw
The Nature of Computation: An Introduction to Computer Science

James J. McGregor and Alan H. Watt
Simple Pascal

Gerald N. Pitts and Barry L. Bateman
Essentials of COBOL Programming: A Structured Approach

Donald D. Spencer
Computers in Number Theory

Ivan Tomek
Introduction to Computer Organization

First Annual
Conference Proceedings

Microcomputers in K-12 Education

Pierre Barrette, Editor
Southern Illinois University

Computer Science Press

Computer Science Press, Inc.
11 Taft Court.
Rockville, Maryland 20850

2 3 4 5 6 Printing   Year 86 85 84 83

This book contains the conference proceedings for the First Annual Conference of Microcomputers in K-12 Education which was held at Southern Illinois University on March 19-20, 1981.

Library of Congress Cataloging in Publication Data
Main entry under title:

Microcomputers in K-12 education.

    Proceedings of the First Annual K-12 Microcomputers in Education Conference, held at Southern Illinois University at Carbondale in the spring of 1981.
    Includes index.
    1. Education--United States--Data processing--Congresses. 2. Microcomputers--Congresses. I. Barrette, Pierre. II. K-12 Microcomputers in Education Conference (1st : 1981 : Southern Illinois University at Carbondale) III. Title: Microcomputers in K through twelve education.
LB1028.43.M5   371.3'9445   82-2522
                                       AACR2

Contents

Preface

Many people do not take the time to read the preface of a
publication before examining the table of contents or reading an area of interest. I hope this preface may be an exception. The reason for this desire is simple. The preface
describes the brief history of individual and collective efforts to share current and emerging effects of new technologies upon K-12 education. It suggests a model that can be
replicated in other places. The history of this model follows together with the names of the persons involved in the
process and the philosophy underlying the Conference.

HISTORY

The first annual K-12 Microcomputers in Education Conference was conceived in the fall of 1978 at the College of Education, Southern Illinois University at Carbondale. I had
newly arrived as a faculty member in the Department of Curriculum, Instruction and Media. A written proposal was submitted through the department to the college to support the
purchase of several microcomputer systems, computer terminals, and other hardware. After a period of time the proposal was completely funded by the College of Education. In
the summer of 1979 the University also supported a mini-sab-
batical for me to design and develop selected materials to
be implemented with the hardware.

During the fall of 1979 and spring of 1980 several opportunities presented themselves for me to meet with members of
the Illinois State Board of Education and the Southern Illinois Educational Service Center located in Marion, Illinois.
Members of the Illinois State Board of Education included
Mrs. Willadene Brown and Mr. Mont Davis. Mr. Larry Goldsmith is director of the Southern Illinois Educational Service Center, an organization representing and serving 27
counties.

Among other matters, we tried in these meetings to understand important issues facing Illinois public schools. During these discussions the question was returned to me.
"What do you think are important issues that face our
schools?" As distilled, the responses offered were associated with the probable impact that microcomputer technologies would have on public education generally and our Illinois schools in particular, regardless of their local or

other organizational patterns, enrollment changes, financial changes or financial support, or the current instructional or management practices they employ.

After several meetings I offered the suggestion that it might be appropriate to consider organizing a conference during the spring of 1981 to bring educators together and provide them with opportunities to focus upon these and other related issues.

The response was positive. However, how could we organize a conference on the basis of what likely would occur, since it hadn't yet occurred? Would people consider it viable? Where would the physical location of such a conference be? Were there enough individuals who would want to attend? Would the interest level be high enough for people to even come? Who would be the presenters and keynote speakers? Would school administrators encourage staff to attend? What were we to do about a budget that did not even exist to sustain advance announcement expenses? These and many other questions surfaced once the decision was made to go ahead with the first conference. There was less than six months from initial decision time to the conference date.

A coordinating committee of Mrs. Brown, Mr. Davis, Mr. Goldsmith and myself was formed. It was deemed important to further involve interested or partially interested persons by forming a larger advisory committee. Several meetings of the advisory committee were held and members were asked for their suggestions for the Conference as well as to search for individuals who could serve as presenters. The committee's efforts proved very successful. Each committee member was able to locate persons who were actually using microcomputer systems for instruction or management. A list of possible presenters was prepared. From that list and from other sources the presenters were invited.

The College of Education at Southern Illinois University made available their entire physical facilities for the two-day conference. In addition, the college agreed to sponsor one of the keynote speakers. The second keynote speaker was sponsored by the Southern Illinois Educational Services Center. Southern Illinois University, through its Graduate School and Continuing Education Division, authorized the offering of a one-credit course through the Department of Curriculum, Instruction and Media. The University's security service made available free parking for all participants. The Vocational Center of the Carbondale high school district arranged for printing the conference brochure.

Mr. Richard Haney, Assistant Superintendent for the Illinois State Board of Education office in Mt. Vernon, Illinois, totally supported staff time reallocation for the con-

ference.   This commitment was further enhanced and embraced
by the close working relationship between Illinois State
Board of Education and their local office in the College of
Education.

   Mr. Larry Goldsmith, director of the Southern Illinois
Educational Service Center, led the effort to provide staff
and other support.

   Mrs. Willadene Brown coordinated the efforts to arrange
presenters from various locations.   Written materials were
requested for each presentation to appear in the Conference
Proceedings.   Southern Illinois University at Carbondale,
through the College of Education, volunteered the use of its
mainframe computers and advanced word processing program
(University of Waterloo SCRIPT) in the preparation of the
Proceedings.

   The conference was held.   An original estimate of 200
participants was overshadowed by the more than 450 final
registration.   Outstanding conference evaluations clearly
reflected the work of each and every person who volunteered
time and effort.

PREPARATION OF PROCEEDINGS

   There were no restrictions as to content or length of the
materials submitted for the Proceedings.   Presenters were
encouraged to describe what they were doing with microcomputers and what effects their applications had had in any instructional or management area.   The emphasis was on practical application experiences.

   The written presentations were keyed most efficiently
into separate microcomputer Pascal text files by Mrs. Janice
Fisher, an office volunteer from the Educational Service
Center.   The collection of Pascal text files was then uploaded into the University's mainframe system by Mr. William
Morey, a volunteer from the Office of International Education, using his personal computer and an uploading program
he had developed.   Draft copies of the uploaded text files
were then generated.   A graduate student volunteer then in
the College of Education's program in Business Education,
Miss Anne Hill, began the time-consuming process of inputting and redefining the appropriate SCRIPT controls to set
up our output format.   This writer received and edited numerous draft copies of each of the presentations for consis-
tency and intent.   In order to make the Proceedings more
useful to participants and others, the writer decided to
build and include an index of keywords, key phrases and
names.   (Most proceedings do not include such an index.)
This index was generated by the University's Waterloo SCRIPT

program. Miss Hill greatly assisted, spending numerous hours entering edited draft changes and also offering and making technical writing recommendations so as to further clarify the intent of each of the presentations. Her willingness to volunteer her time and expertise, even though she had not attended the conference, is noted in every page of this document that was electronically generated. Without her personal assistance, the preparation of these Proceedings would not have been possible.

CONFERENCE ADVISORY COMMITTEE

Mr. Robert Campbell
Curriculum Director
Marion Unit School District
Marion, IL 62959

Mr. Troy Cole
Educational Consultant
Illinois State Board of Education
Mt. Vernon State Office Building
Mt. Vernon, IL 62864

Mr. David Dagley
Business Manager
Wabash-Ohio Valley Special Education
  District
Post Office Box E
Norris City, IL 62869

Mr. Mont Davis
Illinois State Board of Education
Mt. Vernon State Office Building
601 North 18th Street
Mt. Vernon, IL 62864

Mr. John Farrell
Director
Area Gifted Service Center
306 East Church St.
Benton, IL 62812

Mr. Harold Finn
Educational Consultant
Illinois State Board of Education
Mr. Vernon State Office Building
601 North 18th Street
Mt. Vernon, IL 62864

Dr. Allen Patton
Assistant Regional Superintendent
  of Schools, Franklin County
Post Office Box 415
Benton, IL 62812

Dr. Robert Raver
Superintendent
Salem High School District
Salem, IL 62881

Mr. Paul Schlieve
Graduate Student
Department of Curriculum, Instruction and Media
Southern Illinois University
Carbondale, IL 62901

Mr. Tom Stewart
Superintendent
Akin School District #91
Akin, IL 62805

Using a Microcomputer in a High School Mathematics Curriculum

Jaquelyn E. Wood

Fairfield Community High School
300 West King Street
Fairfield, Illinois 62837
Tel 618-842-2649

Fairfield Community High School, located in Fairfield, Illinois, has an enrollment of approximately 625 ninth through twelfth grade students. Since we have exceptional vocational and college preparatory curricula, a decision was made in 1980 to expand each with the purchase of microcomputers for student use. The funds for the purchase were from regular school funds and not dependent on a grant.

After much study and deliberation, the Radio Shack TRS-80 Model I Level II 16K microcomputer was chosen because it seemed to best meet our needs, to accommodate a large number of students and keep the cost low. We were able to purchase eleven microcomputers and place them together in a room to create a laboratory atmosphere. All eleven are equipped equally with the exception of one, which has an additional 16K memory via an expansion interface, two disk drives, a printer, and a modern system desk.

With the aid of many periodicals and books, an instructional unit in programming in BASIC has been devised. Students enrolled in the business data processing class and those in the gifted mathematics program will learn programming.

In the gifted mathematics classes, the instruction of the BASIC programming unit occurs during the ninth grade. In the following years, the computer is used to supplement and enrich the existing curriculum. As each student advances from elementary algebra through differential and integral calculus, the microcomputer is utilized by programming exercises on the current topic.

Students love to play computer games of logic, including chess, mancala, subchase, and mazes. The regular class period does not allow time for such activities so the computer lab is available during the lunch hour to allow students to involve themselves with problem solving activities or independent projects.

An adult computer programming class is offered through Frontier Community College, also in Fairfield. Frontier, a fully accredited institution with over 4000 students, is part of the Illinois Eastern Community College system. The students are adults who work full-time during the day and because of their interest in computer programming enroll in this class, which meets from 6:30-10:00 PM one night a week for eleven weeks.

Both high school students and adults have benefited from the introduction of microcomputers to the Fairfield High School curriculum. Expansion of this usefulness into other curriculum areas is expected in the future. When one examines the pros and cons of using the microcomputer in education, it is easily seen that the benefits far outnumber the drawbacks.

COMPUTER LABORATORY INVENTORY

11 TRS-80 microcomputer, Level II 16K 26-1056

11 Dual-section TRS-80 Power Line Filter 26-1451

1 Expansion Interface with 16 K RAM 26-1141

2 Mini-disk Drives

1 TRS-80 System Desk 26-1301

1 Quick Printer 26-1153

1 Mod 1 Printer Cable 26-1401

1 Set of Student Manuals and Teachers Book 26-2151

11 Dust Covers 26-501

1 TRS-80 System Carrying Case Set 26-500

1 BASIC Course in Level II on cassette PtI and PtII 26-2005 and 26-2006

1 Line printer VI 22-1166, cover 26-507, Ribbon 26-1418

1 Yearly Subscription to each of the following magazines:

   80 Microcomputing
   Creative Computing
   Computers and People
   Computronics
   Classroom Computer News

1 Set Posters

misc Games on cassette

misc Books

misc Cassette packages including:

   College Board Review
   Gambiet '80
   Advanced Graphics
   Text Processing
   Ecology Simulations
   Checking Account

misc Supplies: blank cassettes, blank diskettes, printer paper, disk storage box

OBJECTIVES

Upon completion of the unit in basic programming, the students will be able to:

1. Follow an algorithm in flowchart form and give the output.

2. Use the four basic flowchart symbols in proper order to produce a desired algorithm.

3. Design a flowchart to solve a given problem.

4. Identify the basic components of the TRS-80 and relate them to the

block diagram of a general purpose computer.

5. Explain the meaning of the following key terms: BASIC, BIT, BYTE, K, RAM, ROM.

6. Enter and run a BASIC program.

7. Explain what is needed to communicate with the microprocessor.

8. Explain the purpose and use of the following BASIC statements: PRINT, LET, REM.

9. Explain the purpose and use of the following BASIC commands: RUN, LIST, NEW.

10. List the names of the three parts of a line of BASIC programming.

11. Explain how to use BASIC to add, subtract, multiply, and divide.

12. Explain the order of operations in BASIC, according to the M.D.A.S. rule.

13. Describe how the computer follows the program.

14. List the steps to follow in developing a computer program.

15. Use the tape recorder as an input/output device for the TRS-80.

16. Explain the functions of and give examples of the basic statements GOTO and IF-THEN.

17. Write programs using unconditional and conditional branching.

18. Explain what looping means.

19. State the purpose of the FOR-NEXT-STEP statement and illustrate its use.

20. Explain the INPUT statement, in-cluding its use with two types of variables.

21. Explain the use of and write programs with the four statements used in graphics: SET, RESET, POINT, CLS.

22. Explain the use of and write programs with two additional PRINT statements.

23. Explain the system used for selecting any point on the entire screen.

24. Create graphics on the TRS-80 video display.

25. Explain the use of the READ-DATA statement pair.

26. List and explain four rules concerning the use of the READ-DATA statement pair.

27. Explain how the READ-DATA statement pair can be used with the FOR-NEXT statement.

28. Explain the general purposes of the GOSUB-RETURN and ON-GOSUB-RETURN statements.

29. Trace the execution of programs which use these two statements.

30. Write programs using these statements to make the programs more efficient.

31. Define the following terms: numeric array, dimension, matrix.

32. Explain the main purpose for using numeric arrays.

33. Create one and two dimensional numeric arrays.

34. Develop, enter, and run programs using numeric arrays.

PROGRAMMING IDEAS FOR USE IN THE MATHEMATICS CURRICULUM

Write a computer program in BASIC to:

A) Algebra I

1. Print values of x^n where $1 \leq x \leq 10$ and $1 \leq n=5$ (whole numbers).

2. Find all factors of a given number.

3. Find all prime numbers less than 100.

4. Read the coordinates of a point and tell if it satisfies YLAX+b.

5. Solve equations of the form AX+B=C.

6. Test the distributive property.

7. Compute the distance between two points.

8. Find what percent x is of y.

9. Find arithmetic mean and geometric mean of numbers.

B) Algebra II

1. Solve 3 equations in 3 variables.

2. Solve 3 equations in 3 variables in matrix form.

3. Factor trinomials.

4. Find roots of equations of the form $ax^2+bx+c=0$.

5. Read A for $Y=AX^2$ and print the parabola's focus, directrix, vertex, and line of symmetry.

6. Read A,B,C,D and find the sum and product of the complex numbers (A+Bi) and (C+Di).

7. Do synthetic division of degree 5 or less by X+K.

8. Produce a specified number of terms of a geometric or arithmetic sequence.

9. Evaluate the discriminant.

C) Geometry

1. Compute slope of a line given 2 points on the line.

2. Read the slope and a point of a line and print the equation.

3. Read slope and constant terms of two lines and tell whether the lines are parallel, intersecting, or coinciding. If intersecting, tell where.

4. Solve for a missing side of a right triangle.

5. Find sum of the interior angles of a polygon given the number of sides

6. Input the radius of a sphere and calculate the volume.

7. Find the volume of a pyramid.

8. Use Heron's Theorem to compute the area of a triangle.

D) Trigonometry

1. Find the measure of the 3rd angle of a triangle and the 2 remaining sides if 2 angles and a side are given.

2. Convert degrees to radians.

3. Produce a table of trigonemetric functions.

4. Input radius and rpm and produce linear velocity.

E) Probability and Statistics

1. Print the values of 1! to 20!

2. Evaluate P(n,r) and C(n,r).

3. Find mean and standard deviation.

4. Calculate the probability of 2 people in a room of N people having the same first initial.

5. Compute expected value of a random variable.

F) Analytic Geometry and Calculus

1. Compute and print the norm of a vector.

2. Add and find inner product of two vectors.

3. Convert coordinates to polar form.

4. Compute upper and lower sums to compute area under a curve.

5. Compute the derivative of a given polynomial function.

BIBLIOGRAPHY

Corcoran, Devlin, Gaughan, Johnson and Wisner. Algebra TWO. Glenview, Illinois: Scott, Foresman and Company, 1977.

Dwyer and Critchfield. BASIC and the Personal Computer. Reading, Massachusetts: Addison-Wesley Publishing Company, 1979.

Golden, N. Computer Programming in the BASIC Language. New York: Harcourt Brace Jovanovich, 1981.

Student Manual Part I: Introduction to BASIC. Fort Worth: Radio Shack, Inc., 1979

TRS-80 Microcomputer Sourcebook for Educators. Fort Worth: Radio Shack, Inc., 1980.

Microcomputers: A+ in Business Education

Mary Lynn Wiman

Centralia High School
1000 East Third Street
Centralia, Illinois 62801
Tel 618-244-3320

I am very happy to share my experiences working with microcomputers in business education. The microcomputer can be a terrific motivator for both the teacher and the students. At Centralia High School, the number of data processing classes increased from two to five this year with the introduction of just one TRS-80 microcomputer. Enrollment for the 1981-82 school year indicates doubling the present enrollment.

At the present time, CHS has one Model III 16K and three Model I Level II 16K microcomputers; all use cassette recorder input. Loading programs from cassette tapes has been fairly successful, although the time involved in loading tapes could be better used. We hope to upgrade at least one station to disk and add a network system. Although our equipment has been extremely reliable, we do maintain service contracts with Radio Shack.

The heaviest use of the microcomputers is in our Introduction to Data Processing classes. The Clerical Office Practice class and Advanced Accounting class also complete assignments on the TRS-80's. As a result of a study completed in spring 1980, and in response to student requests, an Advanced Data Processing class will be added to the 1981-82 curriculum. This new class will use the microcomputers extensively.

DATA PROCESSING

The goals of Centralia High School's Introduction to Data Processing are threefold: 1) promote computer literacy, 2) develop skill in operating a microcomputer, and 3) develop skill in writing BASIC programs. (Appendix A contains the course outline.)

The textbook and workbook, Introduction to Computers and Data Processing, from Anaheim Publishing Company, is used to promote computer literacy, to develop an appreciation for well-written BASIC business programs, and to develop skill in writing BASIC programs.

Eight BASIC programs are provided in the workbook as computer laboratory projects: Calculating the Effects of Inflation, Computer Assisted Instruction, Word Processing, Sorting Records Using a Computer, Transaction-Oriented Data Entry, Report Formats, Inquiry, and Airline Reservations. These programs are listed in the teacher's manual to be recorded on cassette tape by the instructor. By following guidelines in their workbooks, students run these programs and answer questions from the output displayed. These assignments allow students to follow the execution of well-written BASIC programs.

The textbook also provides instruction in BASIC programming. The approach used will be appropriate for the new Advanced Data Processing class we will offer. The programs are very professional, including work in BASIC input/output operations, BASIC arithmetic operations, comparing, control breaks, and tables and table searches. Programming assignments are given in the textbook, workbook, and supplementary materials provided for the teacher.

The bulk of the material used to instruct students in the operation of the TRS-80 and in BASIC programming is teacher-made; a sample unit appears in Appendix B. Radio Shack's software, Level II BASIC Instruction Course Parts I and II, provides instruction also. In the introductory course, students will write BASIC programs, including input/output operations and arithmetic operations such as payroll, inventory, interest, sales, and simulated word processing. Advanced Data Processing students will expand their programming to include comparing, control breaks, and tables.

To provide adequate computer time for

our students, our introductory course is limited to fifteen students, who have the use of four microcomputers. We hope to add microcomputers to reach and maintain a student/computer ratio of 3 to 1. Without a computer per student situation, some type of rotation system must be devised. In-class computer work is often completed in pairs or groups of three. While several students work in class at the computers, others review microcomputer periodicals such as Creative Computing or Softalk. (See Appendix C & D.) At the completion of a microcomputer/BASIC unit, out-of-class assignments are made. These are completed while in-class time is spent on a concept unit from the textbook. The course outline lists alternate microcomputer/BASIC units.

CLERICAL OFFICE PRACTICE

Clerical students use the microcomputers in completing units in data processing and word processing.

The objectives of the data processing unit pertaining to the microcomputer concentrate upon data entry and operation. Instructional materials for data entry are teacher-made. Students are to develop touch control on a numeric pad with time and accuracy goals. One of the computer laboratory projects from the data processing workbook gives students the experience of entering and processing purchase orders electronically.

The computer laboratory project on word processing allows students to complete a word processing simulation. A teacher-made assignment gives students the experience of keying in a program and a letter, responding to prompts and editing.

Clerical students also enjoy using Typing Tutor, software which improves or teaches keyboarding skill. The program may be used to learn the alphabetic or numeric keyboard or to improve speed and accuracy. Paragraphs are constructed which measure and evaluate a student's typewriting skill. This program may be used in data processing or typing classes also.

ADVANCED ACCOUNTING

A software program Ledger appeared in CLOAD, a monthly magazine for the TRS-80. The Advanced Accounting instructor plans to use this in her class. The program menu offers setting up general ledger accounts, posting to these accounts, and constructing a trial balance.

SUMMARY

Student response to our TRS-80's has been tremendous, so much that it is difficult to imagine teaching without them. Use of the microcomputer is limited only by your imagination. Microcomputers are, indeed, a plus in business education.

APPENDIX A, COURSE OUTLINES

INTRODUCTION TO DATA PROCESSING

Course Description

Introduction to Data Processing will benefit students who may be considering a career in an area of data processing, students who are interested in learning more about the field, and students whose non-data processing careers will involve the use of computers.

The course will encompass: an orientation to data processing, including terminology, history, basic concepts, and use of a microcomputer; an in-depth study of electronic data processing; and writing BASIC programs for the microcomputer.

Opportunities for advanced training and employment will be discussed; field trips and guest speakers will provide contact with the business world.

Prerequisites

Successful completion of any level of algebra
One semester of typing is recommended
Junior or senior standing

Course Content

UNIT I   ORIENTATION TO THE TRS-80 MICROCOMPUTER

Components	SYSTEM
Operating the System	RUN
BASIC	NEW
ROM/RAM	BREAK
CLOAD	CONT

UNIT 2   INTRODUCTION TO THE COMPUTER
Data Processing Cycle
Function of a Computer and of a Program
Computer Hardware
Careers in Data Processing
Sizes and Types of Computers
Laboratory Project: Calculating Effects of Inflation

UNIT 3   KEYING PROGRAMS INTO RAM

Keyboarding	LPRINT
Correcting Errors	END
REM	LIST
CLS	LLIST
PRINT	

UNIT 4   THE EVOLUTION OF THE ELECTRONIC COMPUTER INDUSTRY
Contributions of Selected Individuals
Development of Hardware and Software
Major Companies
Future of the Industry
Social Implications

Applications of Computers
Laboratory Project: Computer Assisted Instruction

UNIT 5 ORIENTATION TO BASIC PROGRAMMING
BASIC Statement Format   BASIC Operators
BASIC Commands and Keywords   Arithmetic Hierarchy
Spacing of Output   CSAVE

UNIT 6 PROCESSING DATA ON A COMPUTER SYSTEM
Detailed Study of Input/Processing/Output Cycle
Input/Output Operations
Arithmetic Operations
Logic Operations
Auxiliary Storage
Data Inquiry, Storage, Retrieval, Up-Dating, and Sorting
Data Manipulation (Control Breaks, Classifying, Selecting,
  Summarizing)
Laboratory Project: Word Processing Application
Variables   User Prompts
Strings   Scientific Notation
String Variables   Auto Line Numbering
LET Statement Format   Editing
INPUT Statement Format

UNIT 8 THE PROCESSOR UNIT
Main Computer Storage
Binary, BCD, Hexadecimal Number System
EBCDIC Code
Addressable Storage
Computer Instruction Format
Execution of Computer Instructions
Variable/Fixed Word Length Computers
History, Manufacture, and Types of Main Computer Storage
Laboratory Project: Sorting

UNIT 9 BASIC READ/DATA/RESTORE STATEMENTS AND PROGRAM DEVELOPMENT
READ/DATA Statement Format   RESTORE Statement Format
Single Variables   Steps in Program Development
                                   Cycle
Multiple Variables   Flowcharting

UNIT 10 INPUT TO THE COMPUTER SYSTEM
Batch Versus Transaction-Oriented Data Processing
Punched Card, Magnetic Tape/Disk
Dumb Versus Intelligent Terminals
Specialized Input Devices
Laboratory Project: Transaction-Oriented Data Entry

ADVANCED DATA PROCESSING

Course Description

Advanced Data Processing will allow students who developed an interest in or aptitude for data processing to further their knowledge. In order to meet the needs of students interested in data processing careers, emphasis will be placed upon more advanced concepts such as data communications, distributed data processing, systems design, and various programming languages. Students will develop skill in writing and executing BASIC programs on a microcomputer.

Prerequisites

Successful completion of Introduction to Data Processing

Course Content

UNIT I   WRITING BASIC PROGRAMS USING GOTO, IF-THEN, AND STOP STATEMENTS
          GOTO Statement Format
          Looping
          Unconditional Branch
          IF-THEN Statement Format
          Conditional Branch
          STOP Statement Format

UNIT 2   AUXILIARY STORAGE AND FILE ORGANIZATION
          Need for Auxiliary Storage
          Magnetic Tape/Magnetic Disk
          Random/Sequential Access
          File Organization
          Auxiliary Storage Needs Depending Upon Business Size
          Laboratory Project: Inquiry

UNIT 3   WRITING BASIC PROGRAMS USING FOR-NEXT-STEP STATEMENTS
          FOR/NEXT Statement Format
          Loops
          STEP Counters
          Nested Loops

UNIT 4   DATA COMMUNICATIONS
          Components of a Network
          Multiprogramming
          Implications
          Laboratory Project: Airline Reservations

UNIT 5   WRITING BASIC PROGRAMS USING PRINT TAB, PRINT USING, AND PRINT
            AT STATEMENTS
          PRINT TAB Statement Format
          PRINT USING Statement Format
          PRINT AT Statement Format
          Advanced Editing

UNIT 6   DATA BASE AND DISTRIBUTED DATA PROCESSING
        Data Base Components
        Data Relationships
        Data Base Storage and Retrieval
        Distributed Data Processing Concepts

UNIT 7   WRITING STRUCTURED BASIC BUSINESS PROGRAMS
        Input/Output Operations

UNIT 8   SYSTEMS ANALYSIS AND DESIGN
        Data Processing Department Structure and Function
        Five Phases Used in System Projects
        Flow Diagrams
        Systems Flowcharts
        Major Business Systems Applications

UNIT 9   WRITING STRUCTURED BASIC BUSINESS PROGRAMS
        Arithmetic Operations--Accumulating Final Totals

UNIT 10 PROGRAM DESIGN AND FLOWCHARTING
        Review of Program Specifications
        Control Structures in Structured Programming
        Structured Design
        Egoless Programming/Structured Walkthroughs
        Logic
        Decision Tables

UNIT 11 WRITING STRUCTURED BASIC BUSINESS PROGRAMS
        Comparing

UNIT 12 PROGRAMMING LANGUAGES--CODING AND TESTING PROGRAMS
        Assembler Language, FORTRAN, COBOL, PL/1, RPG, BASIC, Pascal
        Compilers/Interpreters
        Program Testing Procedures
        Program Documentation
        Role and Use of Operating Systems

UNIT 13 WRITING STRUCTURED BASIC BUSINESS PROGRAMS
        Control Breaks

UNIT 14 THE FUTURE OF COMPUTERS IN SOCIETY
        Ethical Considerations
        Data Banks/Electronic Funds Transfer
        Freedom/Privacy Threats

ADDITIONAL TOPICS TO COVER AS TIME PERMITS
        WRITING BASIC PROGRAMS WITH DIM STATEMENTS
        WRITING STRUCTURED BASIC BUSINESS PROGRAMS--TABLES & TABLE SEARCHES
        WRITING BASIC PROGRAMS WITH ON-GOTO, GOSUB-RETURN, FUNCTION
           STATEMENTS
        CASE STUDY

APPENDIX B, SAMPLE DATA PROCESSING UNIT

UNIT 3 KEYING PROGRAMS INTO RAM

At the end of this unit, I shall be able to:

1. Use the NEW command to erase a program from RAM.

2. Key programs into RAM with all typing errors corrected.

3. RUN programs keyed into RAM; make necessary corrections if ?SN is encountered.

4. Identify the purpose of the following BASIC keywords: REM, CLS, PRINT, LPRINT, END.

5. Identify the purpose of the BASIC commands LIST and LLIST.

```
+--------------------------------------------------------------------------+
|                                                                          |
|  SUMMARY OF BASIC COMMANDS TO DATE      SUMMARY OF BASIC KEYWORDS TO DATE |
|                                                                          |
|     CLOAD    RUN   CONT    LLIST          REM      PRINT       END        |
|     SYSTEM   NEW   LIST                   CLS      LPRINT                  |
|                                                                          |
+--------------------------------------------------------------------------+
```

Keyboard Orientation

(Show picture of TRS-80 keyboard)

The alphanumeric keyboard on the TRS-80 closely resembles that of the typewriter; the numeric pad at the right resembles a calculator. There are a few differences, however:

1. Since the keyboard is electronic, use a light touch.

2. The Model I microcomputers have only upper case letters; use the shift keys for certain symbols (note symbol key location may be different from that on the typewriter). The Model III has both upper and lower case letters; use the shift 0 as a switch for changing from upper to lower case or lower case to upper case.

3. Use either the top row of keys or the numeric pad at the right to enter numbers. BEWARE! Do not use the letter "l" for the number one.

Keying in Programs

1. Before keying in a program, type NEW and hit ENTER to erase any old program stored in RAM.

2. Key in each line of the program exactly as it appears on paper. Pay particular attention to the punctuation.

3. After you key in each line, hit ENTER.

4. Good programming techniques require documentation. Therefore, the first line in your program should always identify the program, the programmer, and the date.

   The BASIC keyword REM (Remark) allows us to provide this documentation. The computer has no processing to perform when it executes this statement. It is purely informational.

   0 or 1 REM PROGRAM NAME/YOUR LAST NAME/DATE

5. To proof the program you have keyed into RAM, use the LIST command.

WORKSHEET/LESSON 1 LEVEL II BASIC INSTRUCTION COURSE PART 1

<u>Software</u>: Lesson 1, Foreword, Part 1, Part 2

<u>Foreword</u>

1. When RUNning the lessons, how do you "turn the page"?

<u>Part 1</u>

1. What language does the TRS-80 "speak"?

2. What is a program?

<u>Part 2</u>

1. How does the computer know which instruction in a program to execute first?

2. Why are line numbers in a program often in multiples of ten?

3. How do you change a program line?

4. How do you delete any single program line?

5. How do you delete an entire program?

TECHNIQUES FOR CORRECTING A BASIC PROGRAM

1. To correct character(s) in a line before hitting ENTER:

+---+
| |
| Depress the <-- key the appropriate number of times; type the |
| correct character(s). |
| |
+---+

2. To correct or erase an entire line before hitting ENTER:

+---+
| |
| Depress a shift key and the <-- key; type correct line. |
| |
+---+

3. To correct a line or character(s) in a line after hitting ENTER:

+---+
| |
| Retype the line correctly using the original line number. |
| |
+---+

4. To delete a line:

+---+
| |
| Type its line number only; hit ENTER. |
| |
+---+

5. To insert a line:

+---+
| |
| Type it using an unused line number which will properly sequence |
| the instruction. (The computer will automatically rearrange the |
| program lines.) |
| |
+---+

WORKSHEET TECHNIQUES FOR CORRECTING A BASIC PROGRAM

Enter these statements exactly as they appear; correct any errors you make while typing using <--

```
1   REM ORPHANS/LAST NAME/DATE
10  CLS
20  PRINT "CENTRALIA ORPHANS"
30  PRINT "ARE TUF"
40  PRINT "AND MEAN"
50  END
```

RUN and record below the output appearing on the video display

Correct statement 30 and insert statement 45 (exactly as it appears) by typing

```
30  PRINT "ARE TOUGH"
45  PRIINT "THE NUMBER ONE TEAM"
```

RUN and record below the output from the video display

                              Why did you get an error message?

Correct statement 45 by typing

```
45  PRINT "THE NUMBER ONE TEAM"
```

RUN and record below the output from the video display

Delete statements 30 and 40 by entering

```
30
40
```

RUN and record below the output from the video display

SUMMARY

        To delete a program line:

        To correct an error while typing a program line:

        To correct a program line already stored in RAM:

        To insert a program line:

RUNNING A PROGRAM

1. To execute a program, type RUN and hit ENTER.

   The computer will carry out the instructions stored in main computer storage in sequence.

2. If the computer encounters an instruction it does not understand (doesn't match anything in ROM), the execution stops and an error message is printed. Refer to a manual for an explanation of the error message. You must debug and correct the program.

3. One of the most common error messages is ?SN. SN stands for syntax, which refers to the BASIC vocabulary or rules of the BASIC language. In many instances, this error is caused by a simple typing error.

   If you type RUM instead of RUN, ?SN appears on the video display. To correct this error, simply type RUN.

   If the error is in a program line, the computer will halt execution of the program and print an error message as illustrated below (XX stands for the line containing the error and ?SN is read as "syntax error"):

         ?SN ERROR IN XX
         READY
         XX_

To correct this error:

1. Hit ENTER and the program line containing the error will appear on the CRT.*

2. Compare the line with your original program.

3. Retype the line to correct the error.

4. RUN the program again.

---

*The computer is actually in EDIT mode, which will be explained later.

BASIC KEYWORDS: CLS   PRINT   LPRINT   END

CLS: To clear or erase the video display screen.

Use CLS in a BASIC program to clear the screen before any output is displayed. CLS does not erase anything from RAM.

The CLEAR key on the keyboard does the same thing as CLS in a program. However, CLS in the program clears the screen at the appropriate time and clears it automatically.

If you depress CLEAR   _   appears.

Hit ENTER to get the

prompt >_

PRINT: To display something on the video display

Enclose what you want printed in quotation marks (" " - the shift of the 2). The quotation marks are not printed; they tell the computer to print what is enclosed within them.

LPRINT: To display something on the printer

Use quotation marks as you do with the PRINT statement.

END: To stop execution of a program

LISTING BASIC PROGRAMS

Video Display

LIST is a BASIC command which displays a copy of the program stored in RAM on the video display.

Use the LIST command to proof a program you have keyed into the computer or to read a program loaded from a cassette tape.

Scrolling: If the program is long, it will appear on the video display and scroll upwards at a rate which will not allow you to read the lines. To "freeze" the screen, depress a shift key and the @ key. Hit any key to resume the listing.

LIST Variations (# stands for a line number)

LIST   displays all program lines in a scrolling fashion

LIST #   displays one certain program line

LIST #-#   displays program lines from the first designated number to the
               last designated number

LIST #-   displays program lines from the designated number to the end
               of the program

LIST -#   displays program lines from the beginning of the program to
               the designated number

Quick Printer

LLIST is a BASIC command which displays a copy of the progress stored in RAM on the printer.

Use the LLIST command as you do the LIST command. The LIST variations would apply to LLIST as well.

WORKSHEET/EXERCISES ON KEYING PROGRAMS INTO RAM

For each of the exercises: KEY in program, RUN program, WRITE output on this sheet & answer ?'s.

1) 1 REM EXERCISE 1/YOUR NAME/DATE   WHY DID YOU GET THIS MESSAGE?
    10 PRINT "GO ORPHANS"
    20 END

    LABEL OUTPUT   CORRECT PROGRAM AND RUN

                                            LABEL OUTPUT

****

2) 1 REM EXERCISE 2/YOUR NAME/DATE   WAS ANYTHING ELSE ON THE VIDEO
    10 PRINT "GO ANNIES"   DISPLAY? WHAT?
    20 END

    LABEL OUTPUT   WRITE THE PROGRAM LINE BELOW
                                            WHICH WILL ERASE THE VIDEO
                                            DISPLAY BEFORE PRINTING
                                            GO ANNIES

                                            INSERT THIS LINE AND
                                            RUN PROGRAM

****

3) 1 REM EXERCISE 3/YOUR NAME/DATE   WHY DID YOU GET THIS OUTPUT?
    10 END
    20 PRINT "CHS--THE BEST"

    LABEL OUTPUT

```
4)   1   REM EXERCISE 4/YOUR NAME/DATE
    10   CLS
    20   PRINT "THE MARCHING SHOWCASE"
    30   PRINT
    40   PRINT "DRUMS UP SCHOOL SPIRIT"
    50   END
```

LABEL OUTPUT   WHAT DOES LINE 30 CAUSE ?

****

```
5)  1   REM EXERCISE 5/YOUR NAME/DATE
   10   CLS
   20   PRINT "ORPHAN FANS"
   30   PRINT RAISE A LITTLE YELL
   40   END
```

LABEL OUTPUT   WHAT IS THE ERROR?

                                         CORRECT PROGRAM AND RUN

                                         LABEL OUTPUT

WORKSHEET/KEYING PROGRAMS INTO RAM

1) 1 REM FINEAGLE'S SECOND LAW/YOUR NAME/DATE
    10 CLS
    20 PRINT "ONCE A JOB IS FOULED UP,"
    30 PRINT
    40 PRINT "ANYTHING YOU DO TO IMPROVE IT MAKES MATTERS WORSE."
    50 END

    KEY program into RAM
    RUN program
    LLIST program (turn in listing)

2) 1 REM CHISHOLM'S SECOND LAW/YOUR NAME/DATE
    10 CLS
    20 LPRINT "ANYTIME THINGS APPEAR TO BE"
    30 LPRINT "GOING BETTER, YOU HAVE"
    40 LPRINT "OVERLOOKED SOMETHING!"
    50 END

    KEY program in RAM
    RUN program (turn in output listing)
    LLIST program (turn in listing)

3) Write a program using REM, CLS, PRINT or LPRINT, and END statements

    KEY program into RAM
    RUN program (turn in output listing if you used LPRINT statements)
    LLIST program (turn in listing)

APPENDIX C, RESOURCES

Periodicals

COMPUTERWORLD
  Circulation Department
  Box 880
  375 Cochituate Road
  Framingham, MA 01701

The Computing Teacher
  Computing Center
  Eastern Oregon State College
  La Grande, OR 97850

Creative Computing
  P.O. Box 789-M
  Morristown, NJ 07960

80 Microcomputing
  Subscription Services Dept.
  P.O. Box 981
  Farmingdale, NY 11737

Office Products News
  United Technical Publications, Inc.
  645 Stewart Ave.
  Garden City, NY 11530

Softalk
  10432 Burbank Boulevard
  North Hollywood, CA 91601

Softside Publications
  P. O. Box 68
  Milford, NH 03055

TRS-80 Microcomputer Newsletter
  Radio Shack
  P.O. Box 2910
  Fort Worth, Texas 76101

Reference Books
(Listed by Publisher)

Anaheim Publishing Company
1120 E. Ash
Fullerton, CA 92631

Programming in BASIC, Logsdon

Camelot Publishing Company
P.O. Box 1357
Ormond Beach, FL 32074

Accent on BASIC, Spencer
BASIC: A Unit for Secondary Schools, Spencer
The Computer Quiz Book, Spencer
Microcomputers at a Glance, Spencer
Some People Just Won't Believe a Computer, Spencer
Using BASIC in the Classroom

Creative Computing Press
P.O. Box 789-M
Morristown, NJ 07960

BASIC Computer Games (Microcomputer Edition), Ahl

80 Microcomputing
Pine Street
Peterborough, NH 03458

80 Programs for the TRS-80

Hayden Book Company, Inc.
Rochelle Park, NJ

Sixty Challenging Problems with BASIC Solutions, Spencer

Houghton Mifflin Company
1900 South Batavia
Geneva, IL 60134

A Guided Tour of Computer Programming in BASIC, Dwyer and Kaufman
(Radio Shack markets this text at half the price)

Radio Shack, Local Stores

User's Manual for Level I
Level II BASIC Reference Manual
TRS-80 Model III Operation and BASIC Language Reference Manual

Wiley, John & Sons, Inc.
Box 092
Somerset, NJ 08873

  BASIC, 2nd Edition, Albrecht, Finkel and Brown
  TRS-80 Level II BASIC, Albrecht, Inman and Zamora

Software

Adventureland, Scott Adams
  Creative Computing Software
  P.O. Box 789-M
  Morristown, NJ 07960

CLOAD Magazine, Inc.
  P.O. Box 1267
  Goleta, CA 93116

Computer Laboratory Projects
(Introduction to Computers and Data Processing)
  Anaheim Publishing Company
  1120 E. Ash
  Fullerton, CA 92631

Instructional Programs
  Level II BASIC Instruction Course, Part I
  Level II BASIC Instruction Course, Part II
  This is Program World
    Radio Shack, Local Stores

Miscellaneous Game Programs
  Blackjack/Backgammon
  Casino Games
  Dancing Demon
    Radio Shack, Local Stores

Typing Tutor
  Microsoft Consumer Products
  10800 Northeast Eighth, Suite 819
  Bellevue, WA 98004

Textbook/Workbook

Anaheim Publishing Company
1120 E. Ash
Fullerton CA 92631

  Introduction to Computers and Data Processing, Shelly and Cashman
  (1980)
  Workbook to Accompany Introduction to Computers and Data Processing
  Ancillary Materials: Instructor's Guide and Answer Manual, Workbook,
  with Auxiliary BASIC Programming Assignments, Transparency Masters,
  and Text Bank (free upon adoption of text).

MicroADE Model Gifted Program

Darrell Snedecor

Hamilton-Jefferson Counties Educational Service Region
Court House
Mt. Vernon, Illinois 62864

The Hamilton-Jefferson Counties Educational Service Region includes 25 schools, one junior and five senior high schools. The Hamilton-Jefferson Counties Gifted Co-op is in its third year of service. Since its beginning in 1979, the Gifted Cooperative has identified gifted students and implemented differentiated programs for them in 24 elementary schools. Several of these attendance centers are small rural schools containing a low incidence of identified gifted students. Providing adequate services to these outlying, low-population groups is a difficult task with limited resources and staff.

A 1980 end-of-the-year administrator's needs assessment indicated total support for the cooperative's efforts, yet cited great concern for the availability of qualified personnel at each building to work on a regular basis with the gifted children. Rural schools, most especially those having a low incidence gifted population coming from economically disadvantaged areas, cannot afford to increase staff to serve small numbers of gifted boys and girls.

To meet this need Jan Logullo, Co-op Coordinator, and Richard Sanders, Regional Superintendent of Schools and Co-op Administrator, began discussing the idea of obtaining microcomputers and appropriate programming training for the students and teachers in these rural locations. Additional investigation revealed that microcomputers offered a real solution to some of the problems of providing qualitatively differentiated educational programs for this sparsely distributed gifted population. The natural affinity between kids and computers has been demonstrated. However, it was felt that gifted students possessed qualities that would enable them to gain maximum developmental benefits from computer-oriented experiences. The ultimate expansion of the computer assisted instruction program to all grade levels of gifted students within the Hamilton-Jefferson Counties region could become a viable means of delivering quality services to this low-incidence, economically disadvantaged population.

The objectives of this Model Gifted Program are:

1) provide identified gifted students with essential computer programming skills,

2) provide these students with guidance and support as they develop their individual problem-solving styles,

3) assist these students as they develop software for problem-solving in their area of investigative study, and

4) provide a forum for the exchange of ideas between students, teachers and their communities.

Richard Sanders, Regional Superintendent, Mr. P.E. Cross, Assistant Superintendent, Jan Logullo, Gifted Co-op Coordinator, and Darrell Snedecor, MicroADE Program Director, met to select schools that would qualify for services under the conditions of the supporting grant. These schools were selected as disadvantaged on the basis of the percentage of students participating in free or reduced-price lunch programs. It was decided that several more schools could participate in the program at their own expense.

All students in grades 3-8 in the eight selected elementary schools included in the two counties served by the Gifted Co-op were screened for identification for participation in the program. Students were identified on the basis of their achievement test scores in reading and/or math (95% minimum), their rating on a teacher-scored check list (95% minimum) and their IQ score (120 minimum). At this time, 55 students have been identified for participation in the MicroADE Program at the eight attendance centers.

Mr. Richard Sanders, Regional Super-

intendent, mailed out bids to several computer companies to insure that we obtained the computers at a reasonable cost. The computer bids were reviewed by Mr. Sanders and the lowest bid was chosen. Several computers were ordered. The selected company promised delivery of the computers within 17-33 days. Several more schools decided to purchase computers at this time so they could take advantage of the low bid price.

Ms. Logullo and Mr. Snedecor visited each of the participating schools to introduce Mr. Snedecor to the superintendents and principals, to discuss the sequence of the materials to be used in the program, and to make arrangements for the actual computer site at each attendance center. A weekly visitation schedule was outlined and prepared. Mr. Snedecor visits each student one day per week for a twenty-minute period to assist the student with any problems that might have developed. In addition to this instructional period, each student spends at least one hour at the computer keyboard in private computer programming practice.

Ms. Jan Logullo, Co-op Coordinator, made arrangements for inservice training on the use of computers for the teachers in the participating schools. Because the original grant proposal budget was reduced from $25,000 to $18,000, $5,000 in additional funding was sought and obtained from the Southern Illinois Educational Services Center (SIESC) to provide inservice training in the use of Apple II computers for twenty cooperating teachers. The Regional Superintendent's office made an application to the SIESC for a grant to cover the costs of training two teachers from each of the selected schools. The approved grant covered workshop fees and materials as well as reimbursement for the substitutes' pay during the teachers' absences. This intensive, three-day workshop conducted by Creative Programming, Inc., Charleston, Illinois., has greatly increased the interest in the use of microcomputers for differentiated educational programming for gifted students.

The goal of the inservice training was to familiarize teachers with the correct procedures for computer assisted instruction (CAI) with gifted students in grades three through eight. The first objective was to provide twenty hours of intensive inservice training in the computer language BASIC so teachers could learn how to operate the Apple II computers. The second objective was to provide methodologies for teaching students to learn BASIC. The third objective was to develop a cadre of teachers properly trained in CAI who would serve as resource teachers for other teachers in the Hamilton-Jefferson Counties Gifted Co-op.

Inservice training was provided for sixteen elementary and junior high school teachers and four Co-op Staff teachers. These twenty teachers spent an intensive three days (9 AM - 5 PM) at microcomputer keyboards, learning how to program. Creative Programming, Inc. provided the twenty computers, the instruction and the workshop materials. The workshop was highly successful. During the final afternoon of the inservice training, students were brought in from area elementary schools to allow the participating teachers to begin using their newly acquired computer skills. Everyone involved seemed very enthusiastic and eager.

Darrell Snedecor, MicroADE Program Director, spent a week visiting each of the participating schools. He met with all of the identified students at each of the schools to explain the program to the students, answering their questions about what to expect, gathering biographical information on each of them, and administering a pretest on the first volume of the course materials. These pretest scores were then tabulated, sta-

tistically analyzed, and compiled into a chart that represents the base-line performance of the students as they entered the MicroADE Program. All of the students in the program are making progress in their studies of the Apple II computer; however, the rates of progress are beginning to deviate significantly.

The basic programming skills portion of the program involves the use of three sequential workbooks. The students were pre- and posttested on each of the workbooks in the sequence. We currently have students working in all three workbook levels in the following numbers:

Volume I   39 students

Volume II   11 students

Volume III   4 students

The students as a group have been averaging 99.2% correct responses on their posttests, and the posttest standard deviation for the group is only 3.2%. When compared with the group pretest average of 38.5% correct responses and an SD of 23.7%, we feel that the students are making substantial learning gains.

Informal feedback from the community indicates a high degree of interest in and satisfaction with the program. A parents' night was held to inform the parents of the students about the program's purpose and goals. This meeting included a slide presentation and an Apple II equipment demonstration.

The MicroADE Program is now gaining momentum despite a few hardware and software complications and delays. We hope that the efforts of the Hamilton-Jefferson Counties Gifted Co-op will encourage other school systems to consider using microcomputers for the development of their gifted programs.

Special Education Management Uses: IEP's and More

David Dagley
Susan Gentry
Christy Gunnon

Wabash-Ohio Valley Special Education District
Hood Center Box E
Norris City, Illinois 62869
Tel 618-378-2131

Management of special education, whether it be classroom management or program management, presents unique problems. During the last decade, as a result of HB 105 in 1969, and Public Law 94-142, the State of Illinois embarked on a new direction as the Individualized Education Program, or IEP, a prescriptive approach for the instruction of handicapped students. But along with the new direction came increased paperwork, increased demands for program accountability, and increased categorical funding.

For the teacher and the teacher's support staff, there has been increased paperwork associated with planning an individualized program to meet each child's needs. For the special education administrator, there has been a myriad of data being asked by the State Board of Education, and there has been a rapid increase in categorical funds which place accounting demands that differ from those encountered before. For all associated with special education, there has been a rapid increase in the amount of data needed to demonstrate compliance with due process requirements. To meet these needs, microcomputers have been found to be very useful and very cost-effective. The purpose of today's presentation is to show to those in attendance some of the things developed in two special education programs in Southern Illinois to meet the needs enumerated above.

As stated, central to the new direction in programming for special students is the Individualized Education Program - the IEP. The IEP has five mandated components:

1. A statement of the child's present levels of educational performance;

2. A statement of annual goals, including short-term instructional objectives;

3. A statement of the specific special education and related services to be provided to the child, and the extent to which the child will be able to participate in regular educational programs;

4. The projected dates for initiation of services and the anticipated duration of the services; and,

5. Appropriate objective criteria and evaluation procedures and schedules for determining, on at least an annual basis, whether the short-term instructional objectives are being achieved.

To "round out" the IEP, several other components are suggested, including date of the MDSC and names of participants, long-range goals, names of implementers, date of re-evaluation, and others. Though planning the IEP is a committee task, it often falls on one person to pull things together and create the IEP documents.

This writer worked in another state when PL 94-142 was first passed. He recalls how that state attempted to deal with the new law, and remembers particularly the response of the largest district in the state. In that district, a booklet of seventy-two pages of questions was constructed to "guide" the teacher in writing the IEP. Since responsibility for writing and implementing was not by committee, but given to the teacher, going through that 72-page booklet became an insurmountable task for the teacher. This amounted to "stone-walling"; consequently, very few IEP's were actually completed in that district.

The purpose of the computer program presented by Christy Gunnon and Sue Gentry of Dodd Elementary School is to guide the user in writing the IEP. Unlike the guide of 72-pages mentioned above, this computer program assists the teacher in constructing the IEP from notes taken at the multi-disciplinary staff conference. The program was written for an Apple II microcomputer by ix 'Dagley, Dave' Joe Holt (former Superintendent at Dodd, and now Director of Special Education for Franklin-Jefferson Counties) and Tom Stewart (Superintendent at Akin Elementary District). The computer program assists the user in assuring that all components of the IEP are incorporated, and helps create uniformity in the structure of IEP's for all students receiving services at the school.

Another problem which has developed is the amount of data required to be collected and submitted to the State Office. This includes data for reimbursement for staff, and data associated with the number of students and the types of services those students receive. This data is ultimately printed on the state forms for personnel reimbursement and the state forms for childcount (FACTS). At Wabash-Ohio Valley Special Education District, a system has been developed by Dr. Lew Sarff, Dave Dagley, and Gary Sarff, and is now in place to track students receiving services. The system was originally written for a TRS-80 Model I Level II microcomputer, but was eventually rewritten for the Exidy Sorcerer microcomputer with dual Micropolis II disk drives. As staffings occur, a checklist is marked by the psychologist or curriculum coordinator and submitted to the custodian of student records. This person then "calls up" the student named on the checklist and updates the computer file. The checklist which is marked at the staffing, and the data kept on the computer file, is identical to that information required on the State Office's FACTS sheet. When records are copied for the State Office, it is possible then to have the computer compare records, to make certain there are no duplicates. As a result of this system, the special education cooperative has been able to reduce the number of duplicate counts, yet increase (by

500) the headcount for 94-142 funding, by keeping better track of students receiving services.

A system has been written to manage data for the Teacher Service Record and the personnel reimbursement for all 27 school districts in the Wabash-Ohio cooperative. However, this is not being used, because it will not be cost-effective until a majority of the local districts are prepared to hook up by phone with the special education office.

Finally, the large number of categorical programs in special education makes it necessary to move from a traditional accounting system to a computerized system. Unfortunately, for many school districts and special education cooperatives in the State, a larger minicomputer accounting system is too expensive. At Wabash-Ohio, a fairly well-integrated accounting system was designed by Dave Dagley and written by Gary Sarff, to run on the TRS-80 microcomputer. This system accomplishes several things. For payroll, it is capable of charging a staff person's pay to as many as five expenditure accounts at a time. For example, if a person is paid from Title I, 94-142, and local funds, (and perhaps two others), it is possible to charge that person's pay out to the proper grant, while the payroll is being computed for proper deductions. For the voucher system, it is possible to encumber an expense account (e.g., instructional supplies for 89-313) when a purchase order is sent to the vendor; then when it is paid, the encumbrance becomes an expenditure and is charged against the budget, thereby giving the program manager an up-to-date balance of each budget line in each grant under his control. Also a "voucher search" function is possible, in which a piece of information on the file can be searched, found, and printed. For example, if a bookkeeper needed to know every check written to Xerox in the last year, the vendor field could be searched by computer for the word "Xerox", and all checks written to Xerox and every encumbrance yet to be paid to Xerox would be found and listed automatically.

There are many other applications for microcomputers in special education management. Some, such as an inventory system to control instructional materials loaned throughout a region, have been developed and are nearly in place. Others are still on the drawing board. Examples of this include a phone link with all the district offices in the cooperative, and an internal evaluation system built around student record files and staff service files. Our intention at this conference has been to demonstrate some uses we have completed and have found helpful and efficient.

Most important, we wish to get across the idea that it is not necessary to be an ace programmer to benefit from a microcomputer. There are very real needs in special education management that can be addressed by microcomputers, and there are persons in or near your community who are willing to help you, who have the skills necessary for solving many problems.

Note from Dave Dagley. Until our board institutes a policy for sale of software, my position is that I will trade or give away program listings, and/or copy on disk to anyone. Some of the programs compiled on a Microsoft compiler and are therefore subject to copyright protection in behalf of Microsoft. System is a TRS-80, model I, level II with 64K RAM. Four 35-track single density Percom disk drives and a line printer II are employed.

Micro-Mainframe Linkage

Gerald Burgener
Gary Sarff

Wabash-Ohio Valley Special Education District
Norris City, Illinois 62869
Tel 618-378-2131

In the process of developing an efficient cost effective data management system, Wabash-Ohio Valley Special Education District (WOVSED) employed the use of both microcomputer and mainframe computers. To maximize the use of the two types of computers, a linkage between the microcomputer and mainframe was developed. With the establishment of the linkage, each separate system (microcomputer or mainframe) was then used according to its capabilities and limitations. With appropriate programming, data can be shared between the two systems.

The microcomputers consist of a TRS-80 Model I Level II with four Radio Shack disk drives and an Exidy Sorcerer with two Micropolis Model II disk drives. The microcomputers are used for business functions as well as compilation and storage of child data. Statistical analyses of a limited nature are also completed by the microcomputer system. The limitations are related to the individual processing and storage space available to the specific microcomputer.

However, the nature of the data base of WOVSED (2700 special education students) requires substantial space for storage, let alone for the manipulation and processing of that data. For these purposes, a mainframe (IBM-370) has been utilized. The IBM-370 is that at Southern Illinois University at Carbondale and is accessed through the microcomputers functioning as "smart" terminals connected to SIU-C by a WATS line.

Developing a linkage between microcomputers and a mainframe resulted in several unique problems. Anyone attempting to replicate our program should initially determine that the character coding is consistent from system to system. As an example IBM generally uses EBCDIC but SIU happens to output in ASCII, which is what the rest of the computer industry uses. Although no translation of characters occurred in this case, it might otherwise.

The modems (if a hard line hookup is not used) should also be compatible. Similarly, all necessary keys should be present on the microcomputer keyboard.

When receiving large data files we found it necessary to interrupt after every line of data with a process command. Otherwise the data would arrive too quickly and overload the buffer.

To insure compatibility of data files, we therefore entered the data in 80 character lines, the format used by the IBM-370, allowing the data to be transferred to or from Carbondale in a usable fashion.

A disadvantage of using the WATS line was that excessive phone noise or static electricity could cause a loss or change of data. We found the TRS-80 to be especially sensitive and thus came to rely on the Sorcerer for the bulk of our use with the IBM-370. We also compensated for the interference by copying the data over to permanent files on a regular basis. The permanent files were not harmed by any extraneous input.

The advantages of two systems far outweigh the liabilities. By having access to the different systems we are able to match our needs to the capabilities and limits of a system. With the microcomputers we are able to store and have easy access to child data. The microcomputers are also able to complete some of the basic analyses needed by Wabash-Ohio Valley Special Education District. When the need of the cooperative requires a more sophareticated analysis, the data is transferred to SIU in a quick and efficient manner. The computed output then may be read on the screen of the microcomputer or printed out for later use.

Using the microcomputers as "smart" terminals is more advantageous than purchasing a "dumb" terminal for inputting and retrieving data from SIU. As the name implies, a "smart" terminal is capable of interfacing the IBM-370 through several modes. Instead of typing all data entries or using the IBM system to call up previous data files, the smart terminal allows for data to be entered or sent from the disk drives of the microcomputer. Thus, editing of the data files can be completed at the office without accruing large amounts of WATS time as well as CPU time. When the file is complete and accurate, it may then be sent to the IBM-370 for further processing or storage. Therefore the use of microcomputers even improves the cost effectiveness of the use of larger and more expensive systems.

This linkage between microcomputer and mainframe allows Wabash and Ohio Valley Special Education District to handle a wide variety of data needs in a timely and cost effective manner.

Administrative Uses
of Microcomputer Systems

William Clarida
Edwin Tresnak
Dave Lohmeier

Herrin Community Unit School District No. 4
700 North 10th Street
Herrin, Illinois 62948
Tel 618-988-8024

The move to the use of a microcomputer system in the Herrin school system is the third phase of an evolutionary process which began in 1972. From the very beginning, it has been our intent to get double value from our system by using it for hands-on instruction in programming and operating skills at the high school level as well as for a wide range of student record administrative applications.

Our first computer was an IBM 1130 (8K) with which we taught Fortran and RPG II and made a few struggling stabs at scheduling 1100 high school students for their next year classes. Two years later, we had employed Dave Lohmeier as instructor/programmer and had exchanged our IBM 1130 for an NCR Century Computer. This system, which we later purchased and still own, offered more power (32K), more storage (2 multi disk drives), and greater speed.

By 1979-80 we had developed a highly sophisticated and successful student records package which produced tally and conflict matrix, student schedules, class list, grade report lists, grade report forms, attendance records, and an assortment of other reports such as unduplicated lists of vocational students, mailing lists and labels, and others too numerous to mention. All of these were developed and written, or at least highly modified from existing programs for our specific needs, by Dave Lohmeier. We continued to teach Fortran, NCR Assembler, and a Computer Augmented Accounting (Pillsbury) Program.

The preceding comments are intended to show that in Herrin we have a relatively long history in computer instruction and administrative applications, but the move from mainframe to microcomputer has just begun for us. We decided in late summer (1980)   to make the move to microcomputers for three basic reasons:

Financial
- The new system cost is almost exactly equal to the annual maintenance cost on the NCR system we still own.

Flexibility
- With interactive programming and modification, we can utilize non-technical staff for all existing functions. Guidance counselors, attendance secretaries, high school principals, and, yes, even superintendents can operate the system.

State of the Art
- Our students will be learning the latest and most widely used system rather than on obsolescent equipment.

In selecting and purchasing our system, we were aware of the need to develop and securely maintain a large data file of student records.   Dave will go into specifications and choice as a part of his presentation. At a price of approximately $13,500 our system is clearly beyond the usual configuration and price of most standalone microcomputer systems.   This was dictated by our intended usage, size of files, and other considerations. Dr. Barrette--one of this conference's coordinators and hosts--was especially helpful in developing appropriate specifications.

I wish we were in a position to show you finished products on our microcomputer.   The fact of the matter is that we are still in a stage of transition.   We are moving from mainframe to microcomputer.   We will be there soon; we expect to begin the student scheduling run in about three weeks. In the meantime, Dr. Tresnak, the high school principal, and Dave Lohmeier, our computer teacher and systems specialist, will highlight specifics of our existing system and the improvements that are now being developed.   Later, as time permits, I will

describe new applications for central office administrative use.

Herrin High School's scheduling process begins when guidance personnel meet with students to discuss educational plans and course requests for the following school year. Course requests for each student are processed through the computer generating a tally sheet which is used to determine those courses and sections to be offered.   These sections are then amalgamated into a master schedule after single section conflict matrixes have been examined.

Course requests are run against the master schedule until the most satisfactory schedule is developed.   Each run represents some change in the master schedule which the previous run indicated as a trouble spot.   When the final master schedule is established,   those students whose requests still show conflicts are brought in and scheduled by hand.   When these two processes are completed, individual schedule cards and section class lists are printed.

Herrin High School's attendance policy states that a student will lose credit for any class which is missed fifteen times during a semester. The associated procedures are laced with due process, a fact which is important to our operation, but is not germane to today's topic. This policy does require close monitoring of individual student attendance on a day by day,   class by class basis. To accomplish this, we have our computer print lists containing every student enrolled, with period numbers 1 through 6 after each name. These lists facilitate easy tabulation and transfer to the computer, plus they provide a graphic portrayal of any attendance irregularities.

The data of each day are added to the master file, which is compiled on a daily, monthly, semesterly, and yearly basis.   From these compiled data we can retrieve and print individual student attendance records for an entire semester, a record of all absences on a given date, total attendance (absence) figures for each calendar month, and attendance and enrollment figures for the school year up to any given date.

Grade reports are generated from the same class list file as is used in the attendance procedure. When all data are entered, our computer will print individual grade reports for each student, listing each class and grade as well as name and mailing address, indicate the student's grade average for that grade period, indicate the number of days the student has been present (in attendance) during that grade period, and generate and print honor roll lists for that grade period.

As a logical extension of our current utilization of computer systems for instruction and a full range of student record systems, the Herrin School District has joined Dallas, Texas and the Tandy (Radio Shack - TRS-80) Corporation to modify NDF Project SIMU - SCHOOL Financial Projection Methods to run on smaller microcomputer Systems (TRS-80 Model III) and utilize Illinois Accounting Methods. This project was funded by Southern Illinois Educational Service Center and is expected to be completed by the fall of 1981.

DESCRIPTION OF THE FINANCIAL PROJECTION PROGRAM

The Financial Projection Program provides a quantitative basis for certain administrative planning and decision-making functions. With the tax base stabilizing or decreasing, tax rates and bond elections sometimes in jeopardy, and many publics demanding more conservative budgetary policy, it is incumbent upon school administrators to use appropriate tools to assist in the projection of available resources, communication of the various projections, and enlistment of public support for the budgetary programs recommended.

The Financial Projection Program is a computer-driven model of the financial aspects of school district operations which, when incorporated into a school district planning process, assists local officials in determining spending policies, setting financial priorities, and funding programs. The model facilitates the planning by organizing and managing financial data, applying uniform and tested formulas to the data, and providing a variety of options for addressing the long-range impact of decisions under consideration.

The functions of the Financial Projection Program include projecting tax, revenue, and expense accounts using any of six projection methods. Tax accounts include: assessed valuation, tax rate, collection rate, and delinquent amount. Revenue accounts are grouped by local, state, federal, and other. Expense accounts are subdivided into up to nine object categories. The program allows historical input of actual or estimated values, revenues, and expenditures. The six projection methods include: specified numerical change, specified percentage change, historical numerical change, historical percentage change, and precoded algorithm. Predetermined values can also be specified.

In addition to Financial Projections SIMU - SCHOOL, we will be working on a number of other programs for central office administrative use. In no specific sequence of development, we expect to complete management programs as follows:

Immunization Monitoring
- To maintain a listing of students with current medical records.

Investment Planning
- Cash flow management to facilitate maximum investment and/or borrowing benefits.

Salary Schedule
- To develop and estimate cost of teacher salary schedule matrix.

<u>Purchase</u> <u>Order</u> <u>Monitor</u>
- Current listing of partials, back orders, repricing, and open orders.

The systems referred to in this presentation include:

1. Northstar Horizon HRZ-8064K
    Hazeltine CRT - 1420 (2)
    Centronics 704-11 Printer
    Hard Disk HDS-18

2. TRS-80 Model III 32K Disk System

A Microcomputer Based
Student Recordkeeping System

Dave Lohmeier

Herrin Community School Unit District No. 4
Herrin, Illinois 62948
Tel 618-988-8024

```
+----------------------------------------------------------------+
|                                                                |
|  This presentation was the second part of "Administrative Uses of Micro- |
|  computer Systems" and focuses upon  system design considerations in the  |
|  development of application programs by the Herrin Community Unit School  |
|  District No. 4.                                          -Ed.  |
|                                                                |
+----------------------------------------------------------------+
```

SYSTEM PHILOSOPHY

The following guidelines were and are predominant in the development of the Herrin High School student record processing system:

- To develop a system which is upward or downward compatible with student population and equipment limitations.

- To develop a system which may be used by any staff member with a minimum of training.

- To develop a system which is self-documenting in each of its major administrative functions.

- To develop a system which serves both the educational and administrative goals of the school.

- To develop a system which has maximum flexibility for modification by the end user.

DATA BASE STRUCTURE

The data base is centralized in the Student Master File and supported by several Task Master Files and constant data support files. Significant Task Master Files are the Detail Attendance Accounting Master, the Current Schedule Master, and the Permanent Record Master. Examples of the support files are the Teacher Master, Course Master, and the Master Course Enrollment File.

This file structuring philosophy was designed to avoid total dependence on a single mass recording device such as hard disk. As all files are periodically copied to floppy disks, these same floppy files may be used in an emergency to keep the system functioning.

PROCESSING SYSTEMS

Attendance Accounting
- Attendance is posted daily from an attendance check list which is computer generated. The check list is filled out in the high school office by student workers from teacher hourly absence report forms. Posting is done by the use of a student identification number and is screen-edited with the student name for each entry. Also included in each daily posting are the addition of new students and deletion of students who have been dropped.

From the posting a daily attendance report is produced giving students added, students dropped, students absent by one hour, half day, and full day. Also present on each daily report are the current population figures by class and sex and month-to-date average daily attendance figures.

At the end of each month a report is generated giving a detailed list of each student's attendance for that month. Also in this report are monthly and year-to-date enrollment figures.

STUDENT SCHEDULING

The student scheduling process may be divided into six general areas as given below. It must be noted that the system allows several places for updating the master course file and/or student requests. There are no limits on the number of passes of the scheduler programs up to Phase III.

Initial Setup
- Course request sheets are printed listing all courses offered. The master course file is created (or updated) and a new student request file is generated using the current master file (less current year's seniors and dropped students). Incoming freshmen records are added to this file. As students are counseled, the request sheets are filled out and sent to the computer lab for en-

try on the request file. A running tally of requested courses is maintained and may be displayed at any point desired.

Create Master Schedule
- After all requests are entered, a tally report is printed and a master schedule is manually designed based upon request totals. From this schedule a master course/section file is created on the computer.

Scheduling Phase I
- This phase passes the course request file against the master schedule for the purpose of detecting conflicts in courses having only 1, 2, or 3 sections. An error listing is produced and should be examined for possible revisions to the master class schedule. This phase may be rerun as needed. Updates to both the master schedule and student request file are acceptable.

Scheduling Phase II
- An attempt is made to schedule the remainder of each student's requests. In all attempts, seat balancing is carried out where possible. An error list of all students in conflict is created. Scheduled students are posted to the master schedule file.

Scheduling Phase III
- A final pass of the request file schedules students previously having errors into a temporary schedule for courses not in conflict. (This pass is optional.)

Final Phase
- Student schedules in conflict from Phase II and III are manually corrected and entered directly to the schedule master. Course enrollment file is created, class lists and student schedules printed.

GRADE REPORTING SYSTEM

The grade reporting system is a spin-off of the master files created in the scheduling process. Using the master class enrollment file, grade report sheets are produced for each class and sent to the teaching staff. When the grade report sheets are returned, grades are entered as a class, with visual name verification for each grade entered. Grades are then posted to the student schedule record, and verification reports are printed and returned to the teacher. After grades are verified, grade reports are printed and mailed to parents.

CAI Management Decision Training

Thomas H. Beebe
John F. Huck
James C. Parker

CAP Project, Occupational Education
Southern Illinois University at Carbondale
Carbondale, Illinois 62901
Tel 618-453-3321

A project entitled CAI Management Decision Training in the Department of Educational Leadership and Administration started phase one on July 1, 1980. Previous work by Drs. Wayne S. Ramp and James C. Parker serves as a guideline for the CAI lessons. Ramp and Parker developed a source book designed to "orient a student to the requirements and the rationale of a competently performing program leader." Additionally, they developed a Proficiency Development Portfolio, designed to "provide a basic system for competency and performance based assessment, and competency and performance based certification." The books provide previously validated materials for use by project staff.

The materials provided by Ramp and Parker are formatted into computer assisted instruction programs for use on the Apple II microcomputer and are designed for persons not having computer programming skills. The student need only follow the simple instructions pro-

vided on the output device. Instructors are provided with additional steps designed to allow examination of a student's progress through the materials. Interspaced throughout the programs are short quizzes the student is asked to complete. If the student's responses are incorrect, immediate feedback is provided to assist in understanding the material better. The results of these exercises are readily available to the instructor for his/her perusal. Through their careful examination of the responses they will be able to rapidly analyze the student's performance in a given area.

Each of the programs developed by the project staff will be available through the Illinois State Board of Education, Department of Adult Vocational and Technical Education, upon completion of the project.

Computer assisted instruction (CAI) has its foundations in the work performed by Dr. Patrick Suppes and Dr. Richard Atkinson in the latter part of 1962. Suppes and Atkinson felt the computer offered a means to control presentation of material in their studies on complex learning. The computer utilized by Suppes and Atkinson was the PDP-1, a second generation computer, the first generation being the initial introduction of commercial electronic digital computers in 1951. The ensuing years, 1963 through 1969, brought a rapid influx of student participation in computer assisted instruction. CAI was delivered through the use of computer terminals carried to different locations about the country and connected to a main computer through telephone lines (long lines).

The funds available for the developmental work on CAI began to show marked decreases during the period 1970-71. The research monies previously available from the National Science Foundation and the U. S. Office of Education suddenly were restricted and CAI research on a nationwide level diminished. Discretionary funding through the Elementary and Secondary Education Act did, however, enable individual schools to continue with CAI. A perusal of literature from 1971 on shows continued research of CAI but lacks the concentration of the years 1966-70.

Evolutionary developments in computer technology since 1951 enhanced the value of computers in educational use. Part of this evolution gave birth to the standalone microcomputer system in 1977. Apple Computer Corporation, Radio Shack (a division of Tandy Corporation), and Commodore Business Machines each entered the market with one.

These relatively low cost systems suddenly made computer hardware available to every school as well as the general populace. Fiscally restricted schools now had the opportunity to purchase their own computer systems at a fraction of the cost for a full size computer. Once again, as in the years 1966-70, computer assisted instruction

has flourished. Federal and state monies are being expended to develop needed software in many curricula.

One such area, Vocational Education Administration, is currently being researched at Southern Illinois University at Carbondale. The Illinois State Board of Education, Department of Adult Vocational and Technical Education, is funding a project designed to deliver, via a microcomputer, the necessary competencies needed by a vocational administrator. Administration of any educational program requires a diverse knowledge and understanding of the many problems that will require daily attention. It is a difficult arena for the administrator who lacks years of experience and practice. Prior to this time the potential administrator gained experience by doing rather than simulating a situation. Through the use of the microcomputer and the simulation technique the potential administrator can gain some exposure to situation oriented problems that will require decision making skills. Through interaction with the microcomputer the potential administrator is able to explore a variety of avenues prior to making a decision. The luxury of this exploration often cannot be justified in the work situation. Procrastination in the real work setting is both time consuming and costly. Additionally, the wrong decision by an administrator can lead to subsequent problems.

This is not to say, nor is it inferred, that the use of a microcomputer will prevent an administrator from making the wrong decision. Rather, the interaction between the student and the machine will afford the opportunity to err and then examine a different approach to the solution of a problem.

Simulation is only one technique that can be employed in teaching decision making skills. It is, however, a technique that affords the student the opportunity for practice prior to entry into the real work situation. Whether the designer of a computer assisted instruction program employs games, drill and practice, tutorial, or simulation, the end result is always the same, i.e., to provide the student with the necessary competencies to function in a particular endeavor. Potential administrators can be exposed to a variety of different educational situations presented by the microcomputer program in a relatively short time. The same exposure would be available only after months or even years of work as an administrator. Through use of the microcomputer as a teaching tool, decision making skills can be developed and honed prior to the actual entry into the world of work.

REFERENCES

Datapro Research Corporation. Datapro Reports on Minicomputers. 1980.

Finch, M. J. An overview of computer managed instruction. Educational Technology, July 1972, 46-47.

Grayson, Lawrence. The U. S. Office of Education and Computer Activities: A summary of support. Educational Technology November 1971, 52.

LeCarme, O. and R. Lewis. Computers in Education. New York: American Elsevier, 1972.

Suppes, P. Computer-Assisted Instruction: Stanford's 1965-66 Arithmetic Program. New York: Academic Press, 1968.

Pascal vs. BASIC

B. Scott Andersen

Senior, Department of Computer Science
Southern Illinois University at Carbondale
Carbondale, Illinois 62901

Programming languages have slowly crept into the realm of topics that educators will have to understand in the next decade. Computer science has developed new techniques for programming as well as new programming languages that are especially well suited for their application to microcomputers. Microcomputers, however, have largely sheltered educators from experiencing the growing pains the rest of the computer science community has gone through, because they are primarily programmed in BASIC. The purpose of this paper is to compare the language Pascal with BASIC and emphasize the fact that Pascal, a relative newcomer to the microcomputer scene, is a viable alternative.

BYTE magazine recently published an article on computer literacy, in which I found this statement particularly interesting: "To be a good programmer today is as much a privilege as it was to be a literate man in the sixteenth century."

I believe that will become even more true in the next decade because society will demand this computer literacy. Computer literacy is becoming more than a topic of conversation for educators. It is becoming a need.

If a comparison is to be made between two objects, it is important to have definitions on which to base these comparisons. Since few educators hold a degree in computer science, I shall have to draw upon any intuitive knowledge of languages you have to illustrate my point. The first important question to be answered is "What is a programming language?" A programming language is (1) a medium of communication between the human and the computer, and (2) a formal method of expressing an algorithm, or a method for describing the solution to a problem. Programming languages are used to teach the computer to perform a new task. A programmer is a special type of teacher.

Is a programming language a "real language" like French or English? Many dictionaries I checked defined a language as (1) any means of communication, (2) a style of expression. Clearly, programming languages fit these criteria. It may be helpful to point out that most programming languages have a grammar as well as certain semantic constraints.

Programming languages sometimes fall into what I call "pitfalls." These include:

Ambiguity
- A language which is not concise may lead to incorrect interpretation.

Awkwardness
- Though languages facilitate the expression of ideas, it is equally important that these ideas be expressed with relative ease.

The main criteria for comparison I have chosen are:

Explicitness
- Ease of the expression of an idea.

Coherence
- Ease of combining ideas into working units.

Modularity
- The ability to segment logically distinct ideas.

Versatility
- Complex ideas can be expressed easily.

Readability
- The language is easily understood.

These five points will be used throughout the paper.

Programs are made of four types of "building blocks" called programming constructs. One type of programming construct is the declarative statement. Declarative statements are used to describe define objects the program will be manipulating or referencing. Assignment statements are used to manipulate the data defined by the declarative statements. Input/Output (I/O) statements allow the program to communicate with the outside world, whether it be a student using a CAI program or a printer producing a payroll report. The last type of programming construct is what the remainder of the paper will discuss. Flow control constructs direct the program to the next sequence of instruction statements to execute. These flow control constructs will be examined closely in terms of both Pascal and BASIC.

BASIC was developed in the early 1960s to teach students who had no previous experience in the art of programming. It was revolutionary at the time because communication with the machine was through a friendly (I use the term loosely) terminal. Since then well over fifty dialects of BASIC have been developed for a wide variety of computers. Of this variety I have attempted to extract the most common flow-control constructs to use in this comparison. These constructs include:

```
IF-THEN

GOTO <linenumber>

GOSUB <linenumber>

STOP

RETURN

END

ON X GOTO <linenumber list>

ON Y GOSUB <linenumber list>
```

Examine closely the BASIC program in Figure 1. The program is designed to compute simple payroll calculations by multiplying the number of hours by the rate of pay ($4.00/hour) if the number of hours is less than or equal to 40, and give 1.5 times the regular hourly rate for each hour greater than 40. Notice the variable names consist of one letter. I have chosen a version of BASIC that uses no special features of any machine, with the intent of deriving a pseudo-standard. The original definition of the language allowed variable names to consist of either a letter or a letter followed by a digit. Does this restraint on variable name lengths affect the readability of the program?

Pascal was developed for much the same reason as BASIC was developed. Dr. Niklaus Wirth and a close associate, Kathleen Jensen, designed a programming language that could teach the basics of computer programming while reinforcing the practices of sound program development. The first preliminary version was complete by 1969. In 1973 the language was revised, and the version adopted is looked upon by most as the standard for the language.

The flow control constructs for Pascal may appear at first somewhat strange to the BASIC programmer. Pascal has eight flow-control constructs (the same number BASIC has), which include:

IF-THEN (ELSE)

CASE

FUNCTION CALL

PROCEDURE CALL

REPEAT-UNTIL

WHILE-DO

GOTO

FOR-DO

Although the IF-THEN statement in Pascal is similar to the IF-THEN construct in BASIC, it has a few subtle differences. Example: In Pascal the IF-THEN statement facilitates execution of an actual statement if the condition in the IF portion of the statement is determined to be true (BASIC allows only a line number reference for a conditional branch). Pascal also allows an optional ELSE clause to be placed on the IF-THEN statement as the alternative action in case the expression in the IF portion is determined to be false.

The CASE statement in Pascal is similar to the ON X GOTO or ON Y GOSUB statement in BASIC. The expression at the top of the CASE statement is evaluated and the corresponding action is taken, depending on the list of alternatives under the CASE.

Function calls are most familiar to those in the area of mathematics. The sine function can be invoked in either language by a reference to its name and a parameter value to evaluate (the angle--e.g., SIN x). Pascal facilitates user-defined functions with the ability to return a single value. This value can be of any scalar type (character, integer, real, or pointer).

Procedure calls are, with two exceptions, a direct parallel to the GOSUB statement in BASIC. First, procedures in Pascal have full names, as do regular variables; second, procedures in Pascal may have parameters in the same manner parameters are passed into functions (e.g., SUB(1) x).

The REPEAT-UNTIL statement is a looping construct used to repeat all that is between the keywords REPEAT and UNTIL until the condition (specified at the bottom of the loop) is determined to be true. Note that the REPEAT-UNTIL construct assures the loop is executed at least once.

The WHILE-DO construct is similar to the REPEAT-UNTIL, with the exception that the condition is checked at the top of the loop. This implies the loop will not be executed if the condition specified is initially false.

The GOTO statement serves the same purpose in Pascal as in BASIC. However, in the time I have programmed in Pascal, I have never used a GOTO.

The final programming construct for flow control is the FOR-DO. This serves the same purpose in Pascal as the FOR-NEXT statement in BASIC. There is no NEXT statement in Pascal. The number of statements to be repeated in both the FOR-NEXT and the WHILE-DO is symbolized eloquently by the COMPOUND STATEMENT.

The COMPOUND STATEMENT is a collection of statements between the keywords BEGIN and END. This collection of statements appears to be one statement, just as one would call a collection of sentences stated by a lawyer a "legal statement." The FOR-DO and WHILE-DO execute only one statement as their object. This one statement, however, may be a compound statement, resolving any ambiguity.

Figure 2 is a Pascal program to accomplish the same task as the BASIC program in Figure 1. Pascal, at first glance, looks vastly different from our familiar BASIC. Comments in both programs have been purposely kept at a minimum to emphasize that we are striving for the language itself to improve readability. The Pascal program appears to be more easily read than the equivalent BASIC program. The VAR keyword is used to signify that the variable declaration section is to follow. All variables must be declared in a Pascal program. If a variable is referenced that has not been declared it is flagged as an error by the Pascal compiler. This avoids the problem BASIC possesses: the misspelling of variables within the program.

Indentation, so valuable for program readability, is easily done in Pascal because Pascal is a free-format language. Pascal does not need line numbers. The body of the Pascal program is executed by following the flow-control constructs. Notice the ":=" in assignment statements. In BASIC the equals sign is used for two purposes: (1) as a Boolean operator in an IF statement, and (2) as the assignment operator in assignment statements. This ambiguity (pitfall) was eliminated in Pascal by the new symbol ":=" (pronounced "assignation" or "becomes").

The semicolon in Pascal is used much as it is used in English: to separate statements. The keywords BEGIN and END are not statements in themselves but instead markers for the beginning and end of compound statements. (A compound statement is a collection of statements acting as a complete unit. Since the entire body of the program is enclosed within a BEGIN-END group, it is safe to say the entire program is only one statement.)

The payroll program produced early in the paper showed examples of some of the programming constructs in both Pascal and BASIC, but the program itself would be found most objectionable by the I.R.S. The programs in Figures 1 and 2 did not compute taxes. Examine the program specifications found in Figure 3. Although the rates are most likely incorrect, the principle should help make a further comparison between programs with slightly more sophistication than the first examples.

Figure 4 contains the BASIC implementation of the program. REMark statements were included in the main routine of the program to help document what the program is doing. What would happen if the REMark statements were removed? The readability would deteriorate considerably.

Figure 5 contains the Pascal version of the same program. Procedures are defined; nameless line numbers do not appear. The main routine simply references the name of the procedures to invoke it. This increases the readability of the program dramatically.

While it was not my purpose to teach all the aspects of the programming language Pascal, it was necessary to go over some of the simpler concepts of the language to assure a broad enough understanding. Before I compare these two languages it is important to point out that there are over fifty versions of BASIC now available for microcomputers. The definition of BASIC I have chosen for this comparison is close to the original definition by Dartmouth College. Pascal also has several versions available. Tiny Pascal (c) is not a full version of the language as defined by Jensen and Wirth and therefore does not belong in this comparison. UCSD Pascal and the original definition of Pascal by Jensen and Wirth are the two versions of the language most commonly found. The UCSD Pascal is the original definition with a few added items. Below I sum up the two languages.

BASIC did not do well in the first point of the criterion explicitness because many complex ideas were overshadowed by the constant GOTO's and GOSUBs. The faceless line numbers hindered the readability and therefore diminished the meaning of the code.

Ideas in BASIC are easily combined because BASIC has only global variables. Working units are simply attached on the end of the program and a GOSUB references the addition.

Modularity is probably the hardest criterion for BASIC to stand against. There is no way to segregate logical ideas because routines can be either entered sequentially or invoked by a GOSUB. One is never really sure if a GOTO statement is needed or if a RETURN will return to a calling statement. Variables in this portion of the program may affect routines in other portions of the program and thus interfere with the correctness of the program. BASIC fails miserably on the criterion of modularity.

Versatility is an aspect hard to judge. BASIC appears at first glance to be hard to beat for the average user.

BASIC fails in readability. Programs of any significant length become nightmares to debug and alter. Variable names of only one or two characters make any references in the program meaningless. The constant use of the GOTO and GOSUB for lack of other more natural constructs only serves to confuse the issue. It is my experience that BASIC is one of the least readable languages.

Pascal fares much better on almost all counts. Variable, procedure, and function names are as long as the user desires, although only the first eight characters are guaranteed to be significant, adding considerably to the explicitness of their meaning. Eloquent flow control constructs support the algorithm they define by using natural methods for transfer of control. Pascal's emphasis on structured programming techniques benefit the programmer greatly, not only in the explicitness of the end-product (the program) but also by improving program development and correctness beyond any that BASIC could ever offer.

Breaking tasks up into procedures helps combine the ideas well. The driving procedure (usually just the main BEGIN-END block of the program) is usually reduced to only a few looping constructs and a group of function and procedure calls. This gives a much better picture of the working unit than BASIC ever could.

Without a doubt, this method also enhances the modularity of the program design. Local variables allow working units (procedures or functions from a running program) to be used in other programs demanding the same results. Programming is, many times, nothing more than assembling building blocks of already working procedures.

The versatility of the Pascal language is best illustrated not in its applications to microprocessors but in its uses in minicomputers and mainframes. Pascal has grown beyond a user oriented programming language. Whole operating systems for minicomputers have been implemented with the use of Concurrent Pascal and Path-Pascal (Pascal language variants that implement tasking and multiprocessing into the language). Pascal is being used as a sort of meta-language (language for simply the communication of an idea) in journals.

Readability is Pascal's greatest asset. When the product (the finished program) is complete, the language supports anyone needing to use, understand, or change the program by illustrating the methods used by the programmer in a clear, concise manner. Although it is possible to have poorly written programs in any language, Pascal's constructs greatly encourage well-written programs and concise programming methods.

Pascal offers the microcomputer programmer many advantages over the BASIC language. It is well worth the time of the serious programmer to explore this new prospect further.

==

Figure 1
(Payroll program in BASIC)

```
 10 REM READ # OF EMP.
 20 INPUT N
 30 FOR I = 1 TO N
 40 PRINT "EMPLOYEE #";I
 50 PRINT 'INPUT HOURS ';
 60 INPUT H
 70 IF H .40 THEN  110
 80 REM<=40
 90 W=H*4.00
100 GOTO 120
110 W=(2*(H-40))+(4*H)
120 PRINT "WAGE IS $";W
130 NEXT I
140 END
```

==

===

Figure 2
(Payroll program in Pascal)

```
PROGRAM PAY (INPUT,OUTPUT);
VAR
    WAGE, HOURS, RATE  : REAL;
    NUMEMP, I          : INTEGER;
BEGIN
    RATE:=4.00;
    READLN(NUMEMP);
    FOR I:=1 TO NUMEMP DO BEGIN
        WRITELN ('EMPLOYEE#',I);
        WRITE   ('INPUT HOURS ');
        READLN  (HOURS);
        IF HOURS>40
        THEN WAGE:=((RATE/2)*(HOURS-40))+(RATE*HOURS)
        ELSE WAGE:=(HOURS*RATE);
        WRITELN ('WAGE IS $',WAGE)
        END
END.
```

===

Figure 3
*** PROGRAM   SPECS ***

<u>For</u> <u>each</u> <u>worker</u>

   I. Compute pay

      1. Hours*rate for first 40 hours

      2. 1.5*hours*rate for any overtime

  II. Compute FICA

      1. 5% on gross <= $150

      2. 7% on any over $150

 III. Compute Federal withholding tax

      1. 7% on gross <= $175

      2. 9-1/2% on gross > $175

INPUT	OUTPUT
employee #	employee #
hours	hours
rate	rate
	gross pay
	FICA
	Federal withholding
	net pay

==

Figure 4
(BASIC implementation of the program)

```
10 GOSUB 1000                              2030 G=(H*R)+(1.5*R*(H-40))

11 IF E=0 THEN 6000                        2040 RETURN

15 REM GET INPUT                           3000 IF G>150 THEN 3030

20 GOSUB 2000                              3010 F=G*0.05

25 REM COMPUTE PAY                         3020 RETURN

30 GOSUB 3000                              3030 F=(G*0.05)+((G-150)*0.07)

35 REM COMPUTE FICA                        3040 RETURN

40 GOSUB 4000                              4000 IF G>175 THEN 4030

45 REM COMPUTE FED                         4010 W=G*0.07

50 GOSUB 5000                              4020 RETURN

55 REM OUTPUT ROUTINE                      4030 W=(G*0.07)+((G-175)*0.095)

60 GOTO 10                                 4040 RETURN

1000 INPUT E,H,R                           5000 PRINT E,H,R

1010 RETURN                                5010 PRINT G,F,W,((G-F)-W)

2000 IF H>40 THEN 2030                     5020 RETURN

2010 G=H*R                                 6000 STOP

2020 RETURN                                6010 END
```

==

==

Figure 5
(Pascal version of the program in Figure 4)

```
PROGRAM PAY2 (INPUT,OUTPUT);
CONST FICA1  = 0.05;
      FICA2  = 0.07;
      FED1   = 0.07;
      FED2   = 0.095;
VAR   HOURS,RATE,GROSS,NET,FICA,FED : REAL;
      EMPNUM : INTEGER;
PROCEDURE NEXTEMP;
BEGIN
     READLN (EMPNUM,HOURS,RATE)
END;
PROCEDURE PRINTIT;
BEGIN
     WRITELN (EMPNUM,HOURS,RATE);
     WRITELN (GROSS,FICA,FED,((GROSS-FICA)-FED))
END;
PROCEDURE SOCSEC;
BEGIN
     IF GROSS<=150
     THEN FICA:=GROSS*FICA1
     ELSE FICA:=((GROSS-150)*FICA2)+(GROSS*FICA1)
END;
PROCEDURE FEDWITH;
BEGIN
     IF GROSS<=175
     THEN FED:=GROSS*FED1
     ELSE FICA:=((GROSS-175)*FED2)+(175*FED1)
END;
PROCEDURE GROSSPAY;
BEGIN
     IF HOURS<=40
     THEN GROSS:=HOURS*RATE
     ELSE GROSS:=(HOURS*RATE)+((HOURS-40)*RATE*1.5)
END;
(* MAIN PROGRAM *)
BEGIN
     NEXTEMP;
     WHILE EMPNUM<>0 DO BEGIN
           GROSSPAY;
           FEDWITH;
           SOCSEC;
           PRINTIT;
           NEXTEMP
           END
END.
```

==

CAI Courseware Delivery with Micro-PLATO

John Eddins

Department of Curriculum, Instruction and Media
Southern Illinois University at Carbondale
Carbondale, Illinois 62901
Tel 618-536-2136

At present, the two most promising approaches to computer based instruction are, on the one extreme, networks of interactive, time sharing terminals linked with large host computers, such as the PLATO system, and at the other extreme, independent freestanding microcomputers. Both approaches are capable of executing comparable programs, but their respective advantages and disadvantages tend to be mutually exclusive.

Interactive networks make possible widespread sharing of courseware, since the same lessons can be used by anyone on the system. They can support powerful and specialized CAI authoring languages. They can provide online software documentation and support that is always up-to-date, as well as online consulting and personal or group communications. For these reasons, courseware development can be done most efficiently on the big systems. On the other hand, delivery of instruction to students may be hampered by dependence on the network during slowdowns, system failures, and downtime for maintenance, and there are the ongoing expenses of system access and data lines.

Microcomputers are independent of any system and have no ongoing costs except maintenance. Delivery of programs is immediate, dependable, and unhampered by the constraints of large time shared systems, and there are no costs for system access or data lines. On the other hand, courseware can be shared only by acquiring programs on diskette; there is presently little quality courseware available, and developing and programming courseware on microcomputers is less efficient, hence more time consuming than on large time shared systems. Since one of the costliest aspects of implementing CAI is the human effort for developing teaching programs, this is not a trivial problem. Though courseware development costs vary widely, current costs can easily run as high as $2,500 for an hour of finished instruction.

Viewed in this light, the differences in equipment costs for comparable performance between standalone microcomputers and time shared systems is not the critical question. The real savings with the microcomputers is the absence of system access and data line costs, but this advantage at present is offset by the lack of courseware and the difficulty and expense of developing it.

At present, the largest body of available CAI courseware is on the PLATO system, which is also the largest time shared CAI network in the world. PLATO terminals can produce high resolution graphics displays, using special screens driven by microprocessors (Stifle, 1975, 1977). Programs stored permanently in the terminal microprocessor communicate with the PLATO host computer, send, receive, and process data, generate screen displays, and otherwise control terminal operations. By increasing the terminal resident memory, the terminal can deliver extensive programs offline, with all the features of regular PLATO and more. Software has been developed by which standalone programs can be created and edited online, in very nearly the same way that regular PLATO lessons are developed. The lessons then are compiled and downloaded to a diskette, for later offline use (Stifle, Smith, and Andersen, 1979).

The result of this is a mixture of time shared and standalone, with the potential for combining the best features of both systems. A CAI classroom could provide most instruction to students offline, while a few terminals maintained access to the central PLATO system, for developing and upgrading the lessons, storing and processing data, communicating and consulting.

In this way, a relatively small increase in equipment costs per student station would be more than offset by a large decrease in subscription and data line costs. At the same time, the large body of available courseware on the PLATO system could be accessed with relatively little extra cost.

The following observations are based on the author's experience in recoding regular PLATO programs to run offline with Micro-PLATO.

Performance
- Micro-PLATO outperforms online PLATO in both speed and reliability. Screen displays plot faster, timings are more precise, and there are no system slowdowns or failures to contend with. Data can be moved from the diskette into the terminal 250 times as fast as over a phone line. Plotting of characters on the screen is more than sixteen times as fast as with regular PLATO. The full processing power of the microcomputer is continuously available, with no slowdowns or interruptions. Timings are controlled in milliseconds. Screen displays are plotted and changed so fast that sometimes it is necessary to slow them deliberately to keep pace with human responses.

Programming
- PLATO documentation and support are so thorough that even CAI and programming novices can produce relatively effective courseware in the TUTOR language. Using Micro-TUTOR, a subset of the TUTOR language, instructional materials can be developed for offline delivery almost as easily and efficiently as for online PLATO. A skilled TUTOR programmer would have little trouble adapting to Micro-TUTOR; a novice would be better off learning TUTOR first. Recoding of existing lessons requires only a fraction of the time it took to create the original code.

Courseware sharing
- Courseware on PLATO is available to users throughout the system. With standalone microcomputer systems, courseware sharing usually is accomplished through exchange of diskettes; however, programs for Micro-PLATO also can be shared by downloading from the host system, with the author's

permission. Unfortunately, not many of the existing PLATO lessons are likely to become available soon, since some recoding is necessary. An author will have to be persuaded either to go back and make a Micro-TUTOR version, or else to release the code for others to do it, neither of which is likely to happen without sufficient inducement.

Costs
– Based on 40 hours use per week, the cost for operating a PLATO terminal ranges from about $2.50 per hour on the University of Illinois system to about $7.00 per hour on the commercial Control Data PLATO systems. Assuming a site configuration of one online terminal for every seven offline terminal stations, these costs would come down to about $1.15 per hour on the Illinois system and $1.65 on the commercial system.

In summary, through a combination of offline and online PLATO and using a microcomputer, it should be possible to deliver computer assisted instruction which is actually superior in quality to regular PLATO, at a substantially reduced cost, while retaining most of the advantages of the PLATO system. Though existing PLATO courseware cannot be used offline without some recoding, this should in time prove to be a relatively trivial task. Furthermore, development of new lessons should be very nearly as easy and efficient as with regular PLATO; and this technology opens up new approaches to computer based instruction, especially in those applications requiring precise timing and fast processing.

REFERENCES

Stifle, J.E. A glimpse of the PLATO V Terminal. *Proceedings of the Annual Convention of the Association for the Development of Computer-Based Instructional Systems*, 1977, 186–191.

Stifle, J.E., Smith, S., & Andersen, D. Microprocessor delivery of PLATO courseware. *Proceedings of the Annual Convention of the Association for the Development of Computer-Based Instructional Systems*, 1979, 1027–1035.

Stifle, J. E. The PLATO V Terminal (*CERL Report X-50*). Urbana, Illinois: University of Illinois Computer-Based Education Research Laboratory, 1975.

Classroom Scheduling with a Microcomputer

Richard Cole

Benton Consolidated High School
511 East Main Street
Benton, Illinois 62812
Tel 618-439-3103

The purpose of this presentation is to trace with you the evolution to this point in creating a scheduling system for Benton High School. Our current Director of Instruction, Larry Richmond, has been and continues to be the driving force in bringing computers to our school.

We had used the services of Eastern Illinois University to computer schedule our students for about five years. This preceded my moving into guidance, but I did work with Eastern during my first year. There were so many problems due to the distance and time lag and the particular needs of our school that we discontinued their services in 1978.

Last year our Title I program purchased an Apple II. Mr. Richmond and I began discussing the possibility of doing our own scheduling. I felt the need of the teacher's class lists and individual schedules which had been provided by the computer of Eastern. We were

hand scheduling and the process was very time consuming and somewhat inaccurate. Time was prohibiting the preparing of teacher class lists for each class. All changes in schedules had to be made by hand on the student's copy, the guidance copy, and the main office copy.

By this time a second computer had been purchased through the science department to be used for instructional purposes. Neither Mr. Richmond nor I felt we could possibly learn enough to write our own program in the near future, so we talked to Tom Stewart, Superintendent at Akin School in Akin, Illinois, who is also a sales representative for Apple. We told him what we wanted for classroom scheduling. Mr. Stewart had been working with computers for several years and told us he thought he could help us. As I had ideas, I would talk with him and he would change those ideas into programs. We began very simply with a one semester program for this current semester. We were able to print student schedules and teacher class lists while Mr. Stewart continued refining and developing the program. The first run of teacher class lists took 28 hours of constant running. The lists, however, were accurate and did not require the hundreds of hours of manual correction. When we began registration for the coming school year in February, we had told Mr. Stewart to add two operations to the program: a two semester schedule and a system to keep a running count of how many students were registered for each class as we registered them. He was able to provide us both. At this point, we now have a program which will:

1. Enter new schedules.

2. Delete unnecessary schedules.

3. Allow changes in schedules.

4. Prepare class lists for teachers.

5. Print an individual schedule for each student.

6. Give an immediate class count.

7. Give a complete class count of every class in printed form.

8. Allow a damaged file to be repaired.

As new ideas for change or improvement continue to surface, Mr. Stewart will tell us if they are possible and modify the program if necessary. To this point there have been no problems in accomplishing this. Whatever ideas I have come up with Tom has been able to incorporate. We feel very satisfied with our present system, but I am eager to watch it grow and become more and more refined. An Apple III computer is on our budget request for the coming school year, which will allow even greater growth and change.

Microcomputers in High School Business Education

Michael Garlinghouse

Murphysboro High School
16th and Blackwood Drive
Murphysboro, Illinois 62966
Tel 618-687-1652

Microcomputers are presently being used at the Murphysboro High School in the Computer Science curriculum and in the Business Machines classes. This is the third year that TRS-80's have been used in conjunction with the Computer Science class to teach computer programming. In the business machines area, the computer is being used for the first time this year to teach word processing.

At Murphysboro High School we are fortunate to have six TRS-80's to use in the instruction program. The machines used are as follows:

2 TRS-80 Model 1 4K Level I
1 TRS-80 Model 1 16K Level II
1 TRS-80 Model 1 32K with expansion interface, 2 disk drives and a line printer, Level II
1 TRS-80 Model 3 4K Level I
1 TRS-80 Model 3 16K Model III BASIC

This is the first year that the microcomputers have been used as the primary means of teaching computer programming. Before this year we had only three TRS-80's, and they were used to supplement the teaching done on the school's IBM 1130 computing system. This year the students are given their basic learning experience on the TRS-80's and the 1130 system is used for administrative applications.

The student may choose to take the following courses in computer science: Computer Science 1, Computer Science 2 and Independent Projects in Computer Science.

During the first semester of Computer Science 1, the students are introduced to the history of computing. When this is completed they are given "hands on" experience using the TRS-80's to learn BASIC programming, and IBM keypunches to learn unit record and computer applications of the keypunch. We presently have six keypunches and six TRS-80's that we use with the Computer Science 1 classes. The enrollment in this course is 40 with 20 students in each of two sections.

Unfortunately, we do not as yet have sufficient equipment for each student to be assigned to a keypunch or computer at all times. Because of this a schedule has been worked out in the following manner. The class is divided into two groups. Group A is assigned to equip-ment the first week and group B is as-signed to read and review articles deal-ing with computer science. The following week groups A and B exchange assisnments. In addition to reading ar-ticles the second week, members of group A are tested over the material covered while using either the keypunch or com-puter to which they were assigned the previous week. A typical month of as-signments would be as follows:

	1st week	2nd week	3rd week	4th week
Work on machines	A	B	A	B
Read and review articles	B	A	B	A

Since the students are working inde-pendently at the equipment assigned, it allows for individualized instruction. Each chapter in the learner's manual or keypunch book has a set of study ques-tions for the student to fill out as he completes the assignment in the book. These worksheets then become a refer-ence manual for the student as he pre-pares for his test over the material. Records are kept of each student's progress as to the amount and quality of work preformed. When the student begins the next cycle on the computer or keypunch, a tentative amount of work to be completed is discussed with the student. This helps the student set a goal for the time to be spent on the equipment.

The plans for the Computer Science 2 and Independent Projects classes will include continuation of the cycles de-veloped in Computer Science 1. When the students have gained a working knowl-edge of the systems used in Computer Science 1, applications will be intro-duced in earnest. Some applications will of course have been used in devel-oping the student's knowledge to this point, but it is hoped that more real-istic applications could be developed to help the student utilize his knowl-edge of writing computer programs. Some possible areas of exploration would be: accounting applications, business math operations, inventory control, and banking operations. These would be determined by the student's interest and ability.

The Business Machines classes are using the TRS-80 this year for the first time to teach word processing. Students are sent to the computer room two at a time to operate the TRS-80 us-ing Radio Shack's Scripsit program. The system provides the learner with a learner's guide and a set of tape re-cordings to instruct the students in how to use the Scripsit program. We have found that most students can com-plete the first three or four lessons. Thus far we have been very pleased with the students' reactions to using the word processing system.

It is hoped that within the next year or two student interest will allow the introduction of a new course in the school curriculum called Advanced Type-writing and Word Processing. This would be in addition to the two years of typewriting currently offered at the school. If this occurs it would be necessary to upgrade additional TRS-80's to Level II 32K systems to allow use of the Scripsit disk program.

The remainder of the time allowed for this presentation will be used for demonstration of some of the application programs we use with the TRS-80.

REFERENCES

Computer Science:

Wanous, Wanous and Wagner, Fundamentals of Data Processing. South-Western Publishing Co., 1981 (New Edition)

Bux, Key-punch Training Course. South-Western Publishing Co., 1969.

Lien, David A. BASIC Computer Language--It's Easier Than You Think. Fort Worth: Radio Shack, Inc., 1979.

Operation and BASIC Language Reference Manual--TRS-80 Model III. Fort Worth: Radio Shack, Inc., 1980.

Disk Operating System Disk BASIC. Fort Worth: Radio Shack, Inc., 1979.

Word Processing:

Pasewark, William R., Machine Transcription Word Processing. South-Western Publishing Co., 1979.

Casady, Mona, Word Processing Concepts. South-Western Publishing Co., 1980.

Disk Scripsit. Fort Worth: Radio Shack, Inc., 1979.

Computers in Title I
Mathematics and Teaching
BASIC Programming in High School

Richard Friederich
Robert Yagge

Belleville Township High School - West
2600 West Main Street
Belleville, Illinois 62221
Tel 618-233-5070

At Belleville West High School we use the Apple II-Plus microcomputers on both the remedial level (Title I - Math) and the enrichment level (senior programming class). The Title I math program at Belleville West has been in existence for five years, but this is the first year that we have used microcomputers. The senior programming class is a new course that was brought about this school year because we purchased micro-computers. The discussion of our utilization of microcomputers will be divided into two parts. The first part describes our Title I program with comput-ers, and the second part describes our approach to computer programming in our senior programming class.

Our computer room is used by both the Title I classes and the senior class. Both are taught in the computer room during their specific class periods. This approach has not created any prob-lems that we have not been able to solve.

The room is a typical classroom. We have blackboards on three walls which we use for explaining new topics and for drill work. Other standard classroom equipment such as overhead projector, screen and student desks are also found in the room. Other equipment which we have includes one regular size table, study carrels, 4 Apple II-Plus microcom-puters with 48k memory, 3 black and white 12" monitors, one 25" RCA color T.V. monitor and one Centronics 779 printer. We have one computer placed in each study carrel. This places the stu-dent in a semi-isolated area. There he is able to concentrate better and have better performance.

Our basic approach in using microcom-puters in a remedial (Title I) class is very simple. First, we teach a topic to the whole class or a portion of the class. This may involve using the blackboard, overhead projector, or one-on-one approach. Second, the microcom-puter is used to reinforce the topic.

The student is then sent to the micro-computer station to practice and drill the new topic. The principal benefit here is the instant response and feed-back that the computer programs give. Third, the microcomputer is used to re-view and drill previously taught topics. Fourth, we might use a computer program to actually introduce a new topic.

The programs which we use are closely correlated with the topics that we teach. When we are teaching whole num-bers, we use our programs on whole num-bers that involve addition, subtraction, multiplication, and division. This same idea is used with all of the units that we teach.

One of the last units that we will teach is a short unit on writing a pro-gram that involves graphics. The stu-dents are allowed to create whatever de-sign or symbol that they desire. This is a good exercise for the students be-cause they learn to plot points and name coordinates. They also learn how impor-tant it is to be precise and correct when doing their work.

The graphics unit is proving to be a very rewarding unit. For the teacher, it involves telling the students what certain computer commands do and how they can be used in relation to other commands. The students are then given a few sample programs that are short and easy to type. This gives the students a feeling of confidence and whets their appetite for writing their own programs. The effort and pride that the students put into their programs are probably more than they have shown for years. Many of the programs have been much bet-ter than expected. They are examples of creativity and hard work that had been hidden and never released.

All of the programs that we use in our Title I classes, except for one, we have written. This has not been of our choosing. There are many programs on the market; some are good and many are not. We found that we did not have sufficient time to preview hundreds of programs, hoping to find the ones that would best meet our needs, so we started writing our own. This has proven bene-ficial to us. We were able to both meet our specific needs and make ourselves more familiar with the operation of the computer and of programs. At the pres-ent time, we are searching for and pre-viewing commercial programs to add to our library of programs.

The presence of computers in the classroom has yielded many benefits.

1. Great tool for immediate review.

2. Student enthusiasm is high.

   a) student performance is higher.

   b) instant reward when correct (the computer congratulates and prais-es the student by name).

   c) challenge to beat the machine

   d) "turned off" students become "turned on".

   e) some students attempt to write their own programs (experiment to see what they can make the com-puter do).

   f) forces the teacher to recognize the computer as a tool, not a threat or enemy.

Some of the problems that have arisen from the use of computers are as fol-lows:

1. Finding and/or writing programs takes much time and study.

2. More class preparation is necessary to manage class time properly since some students will be working on the computers while others are not.

3. Some students must overcome a fear of the machine, much like they expe-

rience with typewriters, sewing machines, or mixers.

4. Students become overzealous and want to create programs or play computer games constantly.

5. Varied programs on the same topic must be used since some students tire of the same program rather quickly.

The benefits far outweigh the problems. Student enthusiasm and interest, positive attitude, elevated scores, can all be results of using computers in Title I math.

Computers are also used at Belleville West to teach computer programming. This one semester course uses the BASIC language and makes use of the Apple II-Plus system. Students must be seniors who have had or are now taking second year algebra. No previous computer experience is necessary.

This course is meant to be only an introduction to programming. All of the more common BASIC statements and commands are explained and used, and every effort is made to familiarize the student with general information about different kinds and types of computers and computer languages. After completing this course, the student will have little difficulty in taking another, more advanced, programming course even in a different language.

The main text for the course is Problem Solving and Structured Programming in BASIC, written by Elliot B. Koffman and Frank L. Friedman and published by Addison-Wesley. This is an advanced but general book and includes much more than one semester allows. Parts of several other texts, including the manuals for the Apple computer, are used to supplement the teaching materials.

The structure of the course centers around each student progressing his/her way through six or seven programs which become more advanced as new material is learned. These programs are mostly, but not exclusively, math oriented. Each student codes a different program and explains it to the class. A flowchart and written copy of the program are collected. Short lectures, short practice drills and explanations are given between the major assignments. A test is given after each chapter of text material and a somewhat objective final exam checks for mastery of the elementary programming procedures.

A more complete list of topics includes general comparisons of hardware and software, many BASIC statements such as READ-DATA, PRINT, INPUT, LET, IF-THEN, REM, END, ON- GO TO, FOR-NEXT, numeric and string variables, mathematical and relational operators, graphics, characteristics of good-looking output, debugging procedures, program documentation including flowcharts, arrays, subroutines, and sorting routines.

This is the first year for this course. The student response has been excellent. Their willingness to learn and the speed at which they learn are most remarkable. The most frustrating features are students waiting to take their turn on the machines, and having much more material to cover than time permits. There is a real possibility that this course might be expanded to a two semester course, finishing up with an introduction to the Pascal language. For sure, computer programming is here to stay at Belleville West High School.

REFERENCE

Koffman, E. B. and F. L. Friedman, Problem Solving and Structured Programming in BASIC, Reading, Mass.: Addison-Wesley Publishing Company.

Language Arts and Microcomputers

Margie Mason
Howard Smith
Kim Traub

Community Unit School District No. 1
410 West Polk Street
Charleston, Illinois 61920
Tel 217-258-6326

The microcomputer offers an exciting spectrum of possibilities in the the area of language arts. The computer can motivate as well as teach students. It can be used to drill the spelling of words or grammar rules, or serve as a text editor or as a tutor for basic concepts. It can help the student create stories or even analyze the readability of his work after it is finished.

DRILL AND PRACTICE

Providing the student with drill and practice on concepts that have been previously presented to him is one of the primary uses of microcomputers in language arts instruction today. Programs to enhance spelling skills such as Stay Afloat, a hangman type game, or Apple Bee, a drill in which a spelling word is displayed for a length of time predetermined by the teacher and then must be correctly spelled by the student, are common. Another example of a drill and practice program is Capitals, in which after the student is given a rule for capitalization and an example, he is shown a sentence and asked to capitalize it correctly.

```
+------------------------------------+
|                                    |
|  Capitals                          |
|                                    |
|    Enter the number below each     |
|  letter you wish to change.  Enter |
|  '0' when you have finished.       |
|                                    |
|        my birthday is in april.    |
|        1 2          3 4  5         |
|                                    |
|  What should be changed?           |
|                                    |
+------------------------------------+
```

The changes the student makes appear immediately on the screen. The students are then able to judge the correctness of the capitalizations visually. The immediate feedback reinforces learning.

With the microcomputer's ability to maintain records, particular areas which need remediation can be easily identified.

TUTORIAL

Tutorials are used to introduce new concepts to the student. Generally, they contain a large amount of textual materials, interspersed with questions. Usually, response sensitive branching tailors the flow of the program to the individual. The Minnesota Educational Computing Consortium (MECC) distributes an effective tutorial on prefixes. For example, after the meaning of the prefix UN is presented, it is illustrated by a loaded dump truck driving across the screen (captioned "LOADED"). The truck dumps its load and now the caption reads "UNLOADED". This concept development is followed by pertinent questions to check comprehension.

MATERIALS GENERATION

The microcomputer can generate Word Find puzzles almost as quickly as the teacher can type in the words to be hidden and the dimensions of the puzzle. The microcomputer will generate the puzzle to specifications of size, whether the words may be diagonal, vertical, horizontal, or backwards and provide both a master suitable for duplication and, of course, a key, within two or three minutes. It will even reuse the same words in a different version of the puzzle if requested.

The microcomputer can generate other types of worksheets such as crossword puzzles, and match columns with similar ease. It can generate word lists and practice exercises based on student performance as well.

DATA ANALYSIS

In addition to performing the usual statistical analysis that one would expect from a computer, microcomputers can determine the number of words in a sentence, the number of syllables in a word, average sentence length, and other data from 100 word samples typed into them. Microcomputers can determine the number of words in a passage that do not appear on a word list such as the Dale List. Programs exist which can determine the readability level of a passage according to the Flesch Index, the Fog Index, the Smog Index, the Dale-Chall Index, the Wheeler/Smith and the Space Index. Some of these programs allow the user to determine the effect that substituting one word for another in a passage or changing the structure of the sentence would have on the readability of a passage. Such programs can be used not only to match curricular material to the reading ability of the student but also to analyze and improve the student's writing.

EDUCATIONAL GAMES

Educational games can be used to develop logic skills and to present basic concepts in a new manner. Their greatest importance, however, lies in their ability to motivate students. One example of an educational game is Madlib. The computer has a selection of short stories or poems stored in its memory, but certain words have been omitted. The student is asked to supply, for example, seven adjectives, four nouns, two proper nouns, five adverbs, and a preposition before reading the story. Not only do the students identify parts of speech in this exercise, but there is the potential for some real creativity with synonyms. In addition, the students can produce original shell stories for the computer to use in the future.

Another example of an educational computer game for language arts is Animals. The student starts out by thinking of an animal the computer must guess. (The computer knows only two animals in the beginning.) If the computer cannot guess the answer, the student teaches it about the animal by typing in a question which will distinguish that animal from the ones it already knows. This game may seem simple, but as more animals are entered, the task of distinguishing among them with one sentence becomes more difficult. For example, the student may be required to distinguish between a crocodile and an alligator with one yes/no question. Not only does the student learn about animals, but he must learn also to express himself clearly and concisely.

SUMMARY

The art of using microcomputers in language arts instruction is still in its infancy. Already the microcomputer can serve as a tutor, a data analyzer, a drill master, a referee, and a catalyst for creativity. Its greatest strength lies in its ability to motivate students. Its future is limited only by our imaginations.

Word Processing with an Apple II

William F. Morey

Office of International Education
Southern Illinois University at Carbondale
Carbondale, Illinois 62901
Tel 618-453-2605

The Apple II, like most microcomputers, is capable of processing words as well as data. To process words, your microcomputer becomes a very smart typewriter. You enter words into the computer memory in much the same way as you type words onto a piece of paper. However, the temporary memory of the computer allows you to correct errors, insert new words, rearrange words as much as you like without wearing out paper, erasers, or tempers. You can see what you type on a video screen as you type it. You can then permanently store on magnetic tape or disks what your computer has temporarily stored in its memory. If you want a hard copy, your computer can transfer what is magnetically on a disk to a number of different types of printers. In doing so, your computer will put your words into the proper page format with such features as right and left justification and centering.

It is useful to think of word processing in terms of five functions:

1. Entering words.

2. Storing words temporarily or permanently.

3. Editing or changing what is temporarily or permanently stored.

4. Putting the words into the correct format for printed output.

5. Printing what is temporarily or permanently stored.

The way each of these functions is carried out depends both on the computer hardware that you have and the particular word processing program you are using. This paper will discuss word processing using an Apple II with one disk drive and 48K of memory together with a video monitor and a printer. The program I will use is Apple Writer. This particular configuration is quite adequate to handle many administrative and educational chores for a school system and its teachers. With this system, an administrator can develop and store standard forms or letters on magnetic disks for retrieval and modification for use when needed. A teacher can develop and store handouts or tests, then retrieve and update them, without having to redo the whole text. I will now discuss each of these functions briefly as they apply to this particular configuration.

PUTTING WORDS INTO THE COMPUTER

You enter words at the microcomputer keyboard almost as you would on a standard typewriter. One difference is: the shift key is not used for upper and lower case changes. Apple Writer uses the escape key for upper case. As you type, all characters are displayed in upper case on the video screen. However, those characters which you designate as upper case with the escape key will appear as inverse video on the screen. If you make a typographical error you can immediately correct your error by backspacing and typing in the correct character. The video screen displays only 40 characters per line and 20 lines at a time. Consequently, what you see on the screen is not exactly what you will see on the page. This is one reason why the formatting step, which I will soon discuss, is so important.

STORING YOUR TEXT

What you have done to this point is enter your text into the computer's temporary storage. However, if you turn the computer off at this point, every thing you have entered will be destroyed. With this configuration you can destroy in a wink twelve or more pages of your very hard work. As you can imagine, an accident is possible. Consequently, it is advisable to save what you have typed by copying it to a magnetic disk. This is easily done in a few seconds. What is more important, after copying, your text still remains in temporary storage so you can continue working. In fact, you can save what you

are writing in the computer's temporary storage as often as you want and your program will simply replace what was on the disk with the more complete version in your computer. I try to save each page as I type it in to avoid gnashing teeth over a loss of an hour of hard work.

EDITING YOUR COPY

Suppose that last night you wrote an inspired handout. You put it aside until today and you decide to go back and see if what seemed clear last night seems as brilliant after a good night's sleep. You can get your disk and load your words back into the computer for editing. During editing you can insert words, sentences or whole paragraphs and the computer will magically make room while readjusting all the rest of the text. Perhaps you decide to rearrange paragraphs within your document. The word processing program of the microcomputer will do this too, if you give it the right instructions.

One of the most useful of the computer's abilities is that of searching for a word or words. Suppose you are editing a test and you want to make a change to question 34. You can ask your computer to search for 34, and 34 will immediately appear on the screen for editing. Or suppose you have consistently misspelled a word in a letter to parents! Your computer will step through your text, look for all cases of the misspelled word, and, with the proper instructions, will replace all misspelled words with the correct spelling. I find the search command useful for many different editing functions.

FORMATTING

I have already explained that one drawback with most word processing programs on inexpensive microcomputers is that what you see on the screen, especially in terms of the position of the letters, is probably not the same as what will be finally printed out on a hard copy. You need some way to tell your computer what size paper to print on, how to set margins, whether to single or double space, and what kind of printer will print your text. In addition, you can change the format within a text to do things like

>   automatic centering
>   of several lines of text
>   or just one line
>   as you please.

You can also do such things as automatically indenting both the left and right margins, and right and left justification, as you see in this publication. However, the justify mode can be awkward because the Apple Write word processor cannot hyphenate big words, so it leaves very large spaces in some of the lines.

PRINTING

Much of what you do depends on the capability of your printer. This is a new topic and to do it justice would require another paper at least this long. Printer technology is changing at least as rapidly as the microcomputers themselves. A few months ago, the small microcomputer user on a limited budget had to trade off speed and price for print quality. I own a Paper Tiger dot matrix printer which I used to develop this paper. I bought it new in early 1980. Today I can buy a printer which is just as fast, less expensive, which will do letter quality printing as well as such exotic things as underscore and superscript. All of this is possible today for less than $1000 for the printer. Who knows what tomorrow will bring? Such a printer could be used in a school to print tests, handouts, reports, letters, and for multiple copies.

SUMMARY

In this paper I have briefly covered one word processing hardware configuration and one program which should fit the needs of many educators. (Apple also has a fine mailing program called Apple Post which would make maintenance and printing of mailing lists an easy task.) However, there are modifications to the basic Apple hardware configuration and other word processing programs which add convenience and flexibility to word processing. For example, there are several plug-in modules for the Apple to make the video capable of displaying 80 columns and 20 lines of text in true upper and lower case so that what you see is more like what you will get from the printer. Each hardware modification unfortunately usually requires a new software program to make use of the increased capability. And of course all of that means more money. For further study I recommend you read an article which compares several configurations. One such article is "Word Processing Software Roundup" by Steven Jong on pages 26-29 in the January 81 issue of *Personal Computing*.

REFERENCE

Jong, S. Word Processing Software Roundup. *Personal Computing*, January 1981, 26-29.

The Use of Microcomputers in Title I Elementary Reading

Marty McWhorter

Cobden Unit School
Appleknocker Road
Cobden, Illinois 62920
Tel 618-893-2311

The Cobden Unit School Title I Reading and Math Program purchased four Apple II Plus microcomputers in September, 1980. Two microcomputers were placed in each of the two Title I rooms.

Using the six instructional manuals and the assistance of Tom Stewart, Akin, Illinois, the two Title I teachers received hands-on instruction in the use of the Apple II Plus microcomputers.

The Shell Games Education Series was used to instruct the Reading students in how to use the computer. Within a week, each of the fifty-nine Reading students was able to turn on, run, and turn off the computers. It was then time to begin serious instruction.

At this time, Reading materials for a computer are a low priority for commercial publishing companies, with Math as their top priority. Apple Grammar and Critical Reading are the only two computer software products we purchased from commercial companies.

Apple Grammar, by Tom Ankofski, published by Educational Software Professionals, is written for the purpose of providing instruction and reinforcement of skills in the use of seven parts of speech. They are: nouns, pronouns, verbs, adverbs, adjectives, prepositions, and conjunctions. The 13-sector disk comes with thirty-five example and test sentences. It requires a 32K memory, Applesoft, and a desk drive.

A teacher using the Apple Grammar can choose and enter any name, delete example sentences, or modify the examples. At the end of each test sentence, the student is given either a happy face or a sad face with an example and an appropriate explanation given. At the end of the drill, the results flash on the screen indicating the number correct out of the total number of sentences, and a percentile is given.

The program may be stopped at any time by typing QUIT and at that point it will grade and report the results.

This particular program has been used with the Reading students in the fourth, fifth, and sixth grade classes. In addition, a sheet of definitions has been provided for the students to use alongside the computer for reference.

The second commercial reading program purchased was <u>Individualized Learning System for Teaching Critical Reading</u> This product was marketed in 1979 by Instructional Micro Systems. However, that company sold the Critical Reading Program to Borg Warner.

The course material for Critical Reading is geared to persons in a wide range of reading levels from third grade upward. It is designed to teach upper elementary students how to use basic logical inference rules. The reading materials vary from simple two-sentence "stories" to longer paragraphs. Each rule of logic is first taught in the simplest setting, gradually becoming more complex. A controlled vocabulary is employed to help the students reach the logical decision whether the statements are true, false, or unanswerable without additional information.

Pretests are provided on each of the three floppy disks in order to pinpoint the exact level at which each student should begin. Posttests at the end of each level are provided so the student's progress and achievement percentage can be recorded.

Students are required to master a logical inference rule by using it in the following three ways:

1. Make or delete valid deduction.

2. Detect statements which are contrary to other statements.

3. Detect invalid use of the rules of inference.

Three disks are included in the Critical Reading package. Each has four level of difficulty, two are pretests and two posttests. The package also includes an IMS chip [1] for Learning. It is a small plug which fits into the game socket of the Apple II Plus computer. This key enhances the computer's instructional ability without affecting its operation by playing a tune when the program is loaded and again when the student answers correctly. The only disadvantage of having the small plug placed in the game socket is that it is inconvenient to remove it when wanting to use the game controls.

The materials used in <u>Critical Reading</u> were originally published as a series of workbooks by Ann Arbor Publishers, Worthington, Ohio. Because of their success, they were adapted and developed by the IMS into a computerized instructional system. Included in the teacher's manual is an evaluation of the success of these materials. A complete review of the research by George F. Lowerre and Joseph M. Scandura, published in <u>Reading Research Quarterly</u>, is referred to in the teacher's manual.

In order to provide equal time for all the Title I Reading students on the two Apple II Plus computers, two System 80's, the Alphamaster, and individual instruction according to needed skill development, a schedule was set up for each group of students. All students are from grades two through six. Each classroom teacher selects a half-hour time slot for the Reading students. The Title I class is limited to a maximum of six to eight students per half-hour period. The students receive instruction four days per week. The off day provides time for the instructor to select and schedule activities for that class. Many times that half-hour works to help the classroom teacher, who may schedule Music, PE or Library for that one day.

The Title I Reading is provided in addition to classroom instruction, not in place of it. All students are selected for instruction according to four standards: Previous known difficulties, results of standardized achievement tests, referrals by classroom teachers, and parent requests. Final selection is made by the Title I instructor. Pretests and posttests are administered each year to determine gains made by the students. These results are available to the Title I compliance monitoring teams and sent yearly with our final reports.

In addition to instruction provided by computers and teaching machines, individualized instruction on specific skills is the basis of the Title I Program. A series of textbooks are housed in the Title I Reading Room providing many levels of reading for each student. Each week a story is assigned and scheduled for the following week. The students' comprehension is tested before they read aloud. Phonic skills are evaluated and the necessary skills retaught in order to meet the needs individually of each student. Comprehension worksheets are also included weekly in order to further develop that particular skill. With all these in mind, covering all of them and providing equal instruction on the computers and teaching machines took a set schedule, which was designed around the number of students in each class and the number of skills they needed to develop. In addition to management of activities, it records of time spent on each computer.

For further computer management instruction, we are planning to adopt a National Diffusion Network Program designed to assist in diagnosing and prescription of Reading and Math skills. It will also pretest and posttest, provide skill breakdown, individual educational plans, and daily update of individual progress. Individual educational plans are developed around the previously purchased materials in the Title I room.

To aid in the development of word attack skills at the early elementary level, we have written eight computer assisted instructional programs. Four of these programs are complete: Vowels, S or K, K or CK, and G or J. The other four programs will be completed and field tested soon. These were written on the Apple II Plus with the needs of the Title I students in mind.

The Reading students have found the programs reward them with a happy smile when a correct answer is given and a frown when an incorrect answer is given. The correct answer automatically is displayed with the frown. Each of these computer assisted word attack programs is introduced with the phonic rules pertaining to that skill. The program may be stopped at any time by typing QUIT and the student's work is automatically scored and the results displayed. All of the completed programs have been field tested by the Title I Reading students, grades two through six, at the Cobden Elementary School. Changes were made as a result of these observations and then again the revised programs were tested by the students.

Student response to the addition of the Apple II Plus in our Title I Program has been fantastic. They were excited and anxious to begin instruction. The schedules are checked daily in order for them to see when they are again scheduled for computer time. If a student is absent, another quickly volunteers to take his place at the computer. The ready acceptance of the Apple II as a medium of instruction, even by the very young, is a sign of the future for microcomputers in education.

REFERENCES

Ankofski, T. Apple Grammar. Educational Software Professionals.

Lowerre, G. F.and J. M. Scandura. Development and Evaluation of Conceptually Based Materials for Diagnostic Testing and Instruction in Critical Reading Based on Logical Inference. Reading Research Quarterly, IX:3 (1973-74).

NOTE

1. IMS chip.   A tiny chip supplied by Instructional Micro Systems. This chip is used to activate the music sounds recorded in the program.

Microcomputers and Career Awareness K-8

Andrew Mihelich

Joliet Junior College
1216 Houbolt Ave.
Joliet, Illinois 60436
Tel 815-729-9020

"What is the Career Guidance Center doing at the K-8 level? All of your services seem to be geared to high schools." These were comments made by grade school personnel before the Region 10 Career Guidance Center implemented its Microcomputers and Career Guidance Project.

"You only serve the grade schools." "The Career Guidance Center needs to do more at the high school level." These were comments made by high school personnel after the Region 10 Career Guidance Center implemented its Microcomputers and Career Guidance Project.

Although the services of the Career Guidance Center to high schools did not change and the direction of the Center still remained the same, the image of the Center was dramatically changed by microcomputers. The Center's image seemed to change overnight from one of not serving K-8 needs to one of serving only K-8 needs. Simply, the Microcomputers and Career Guidance Project worked too well. The project has proven to be one of the Center's most visible, cost effective, and demanded services.

To assist local educational agencies and community based organizations in the development and implementation of career guidance programs and services, the Microcomputers and Career Guidance project was piloted in the spring of 1979. The intent of the project was threefold: first, to acquaint students with career guidance concepts through a hands-on approach using a microcomputer; second, to acquaint students with basic components and procedures of the microcomputer; and third, to provide classroom teachers with exposure to uses of the microcomputer in the classroom for career guidance activities and basic skill development. When the project began it consisted of one Radio Shack TRS-80 Model I Level II

Microcomputer System. Pencil and paper career awareness/career exploration activities developed by the Illinois State Board of Education were programmed in BASIC computer language for use with the microcomputer. Eight programmed activities were originally produced from the Uncomplicated Elementary Career Education System for the "Real" Classroom and the K-3, 4-6, 7-8 Handbook publications. All programmed activities were geared towards the K-8 level. Five elementary schools were selected to test the project. Based upon positive feedback and highly favorable evaluations by both teachers and students, it was decided to offer the project again for the 1979-80 school year and expand the number of program activities. During the summer of 1979 four additional activities were added to the tape library.

In anticipation of a high demand on the part of schools within the Region 10 Career Guidance Center area, a second TRS-80 microcomputer was added to the project. When the project was offered in the fall of 1979, demand exceeded supply. At this point, it was determined that additional program activities and a third microcomputer were needed to meet demand. In the spring of 1980 twelve additional program activities and a third TRS-80 microcomputer were added to the project. During this second year of operation, there were 39 schools and agencies participating in the project.

Each school in the project reserves one of the microcomputers at the beginning of the school year on a first come, first serve basis. Reservations are made through the Region 10 Career Guidance Center. Length of time an individual school or district has a microcomputer is determined by the Career Guidance Center and depends upon the total number of requests, size of schools, and number of interested users at each school. The microcomputer is delivered and picked up by the Career Guidance Center. Inservice training is provided for interested teachers, counselors, ad-ministrators, library and media personnel when equipment is delivered. All the necessary computer equipment, all the programmed activities on individual cassette tapes, and an appropriate number of Teacher's Guides are provided as part of the project.

During the summer of 1980, eight additional program activities were added to the tape library. Again, when the project was offered in the fall of 1980, demand exceeded supply. Forty-six schools requested to participate in the project for the 1980-81 school year, but only 43 could be scheduled.

Based upon this continued interest and success, the Region 10 Career Guidance Center has already made plans to further expand the program activities and offer them to other Career Guidance Centers and Local Educational Agencies throughout the State.

This Microcomputers and Career Guidance Project is offered as a free service by the Region 10 Career Guidance Center with no liability or commitment required on the part of participating schools and agencies. The Region 10 Career Guidance Center is located at Joliet Junior College and serves the four counties of Will, Grundy, Kendall, and Kankakee. The Center is funded by the Illinois State Board of Education and is one of nineteen centers throughout the state.

Software developed by the Career Guidance Center network is available for duplication. There is no cost to schools in Illinois for duplicating the programmed activities themselves at the Region 10 Career Guidance Center.

For additional information contact:

Andrew L. Mihelich, Director
Region 10 Career Guidance Center
Joliet Junior College
1216 Houbolt Ave.
Joliet, IL 60436

Computers in the
Schools: Some Interesting Choices

Ted Perry

San Juan Unified School District
6141 Sutter Street
Carmichael, California 95608
Tel 916-944-3650

As computers become prevalent in the educational setting, the educator is presented with a large number of alternatives. The capabilities of the computer in general are vast, but the alternatives themselves are questions. Which system meets your specific needs? Should you look at hardware or software first? Does any system provide what you want? How will the programs you need be developed? These questions are not trivial and necessitate careful consideration.

CHOOSING A COMPUTER

Two important factors to consider when beginning Computer Assisted Instruction (CAI) are finding appropriate hardware and software. By hardware we mean the computer itself, the equipment that is the computer. Many questions need to be answered before selecting a particular machine. How much does it cost? Is it reliable? Does it provide enough flexibility?

The second factor, software, is the more important. By software we mean the programs or actual lesson materials available for a particular machine. Again there are many questions to

consider. Does it do more than math drill and practice? Are programs at the appropriate level for our students? Can teachers easily modify or add to the current software? The following information may help give you some insight into answering these questions.

HARDWARE

1. Time-shared Systems

In the past five years many changes have taken place in the hardware which is available for educators interested in utilizing Computer Assisted Instruction. Previously the only option was a time-shared system, which consists of a central processing unit (CPU), multiplexor, a hard disk system (storage), telephone hookups (modems), and terminals (keyboards).

One advantage of a time-shared computer is that it allows users to share the central processing unit and the disk drives, which tend to be the most expensive components of this computer system. Another advantage to time-shared is that it allows all the terminals connected to have access to the same programs from

89

the central disk storage.   This connection or dependence upon a central processing unit is also a vulnerability; if the CPU fails, all of the dependent terminals become inoperable.

Although many large school districts already have a centralized computer system for business functions, the high cost of terminals and telephone connections prohibit the use of the computer for educational functions.   In addition, the system's dependence on telephone connections necessitates locating the computer terminals in one central place, thus limiting the flexibility of the system.   Terminals cannot be located in individual classrooms.

The time-shared system is further limited because the central processing unit's computing power is being used to run multiple terminals, and therefore, cannot provide important features that educators want, such as color graphics, animation and voice and sound production.   Difficulties with time-shared systems have led us to investigate the use of microcomputers.

2. Microcomputers

Recent technological changes have facilitated the development of the microcomputer.   The microcomputer is a small self-contained computer system with its own CPU, terminal and storage system. Since it is self contained, it requires no telephone connections and can be set up in any location.   The fact that the whole computer system costs only slightly more than a terminal itself in a time-shared system makes it adaptable and affordable for the educational setting.

Not only is the microcomputer less expensive and more portable, but it gives the user the features missing in the time-shared system; namely, color graphics, animation and sound production.   The microcomputer is less expensive, portable, and can do more complex tasks than the time-shared system.

The main drawback of the micro is that since each computer is independent it requires its own storage system. Thus if a school has twenty computers, a copy of each disk containing software has to be made for each computer.   That is the only way all of the computers will have access to the same information.

Keeping track of student responses to computerized lessons with independent microcomputers may become difficult. The information about any individual student could be on any of the student disks.   This often necessitates hiring someone to keep track of student disks, and to make sure that teachers have easy access to student information.

3. Networked Microcomputers

The solution to the problem of access to software and student records is solved by a compromise between the independent microcomputer and the fully integrated time-shared system.   This compromise is sometimes called a networked microcomputer system.   The computing power of this system is distributed through the use of microcomputers; however, unlike independent microcomputers, they share a central disk storage system.

This system not only allows all of the microcomputers access to central storage, but if a school has a large number of computers it is less expensive than purchasing individual mini-disk drives for each microcomputer, so the microcomputer network system has the advantage of using the low cost, high powered microcomputer with graphics capabilities, while still having a central storage system.

As with any solution, this too has a drawback.   Some of the flexibility offered by the independent microcomputer is lost.   The computers must be connected to the central disk system which means cables must be laid to each location where a computer will be used, thus limiting the portability of the machine.

In an educational setting where a computer laboratory is to be established, the networked microcomputer is ideal. Independent microcomputers, however, are more suitable if the computers are to be placed in individual classrooms around the school or if they are to be shared by more than one classroom The situation must be evaluated at each site.

SOFTWARE

The discussion and decision as to what type of hardware to purchase is an important one. However, nothing is more important than the amount and type of good educational software available to that system. Since software from one computer rarely runs on another, care must be taken that appropriate software is available or can be written for the machine you choose. Generally, there are three basic types of software available.

1. Canned Software

The first type is commercially developed, canned programs. As with already existing textbooks purchased from publishing companies, the content of this material cannot be altered in any way by the local teacher. It therefore must be used in the form provided.

The advantages of this type of software are its cost effectiveness and ease of use. The material can be bought at a relatively low price per copy since the software house or publisher expects to sell many copies. Such software is written in subject areas that are widely taught at a large number of schools. Examples of material with general appeal are drill and practice on math facts or vocabulary development programs.

This type of program is generally easy to use, since it requires no input on the teacher's part. No special training is required of the teacher. All the teacher needs to know is how to turn on the computer and start the program running.

Some software in this category has the additional advantage of a student management system. This system keeps track of student progress on particular lessons and in some cases will prescribe additional work, either on the computer or from other learning aids. Again this adds to the ease of use of this software.

The problem with this type of program arises when a teacher does not feel the software presents information appropriate to the needs of a particular class or student. There is no way to change or add to the material in the program itself. The teacher either uses the computer lessons as they are or cannot use the software at all. This flaw is the major drawback of canned software.

While canned programs offer many advantages they cannot alone provide the most effective CAI system for a school or individual. The weakness of this software is its lack of adaptability to specific student needs.

2. Teacher Developed Software

The most obvious solution to the problem of software adaptability is to provide programming expertise to the teacher using programming languages such as BASIC, Pascal or PILOT[1]. This can be done either by training the teacher to program or by allowing the teacher to work with a programmer. In either case the teacher becomes the author of new educational software, which can be adapted at the school site.

This kind of software has the advantage that it is written and modified to the specifications of the teacher. New software can be written as new applications are found. Using this approach software can be written which has all of the benefits of canned software, while having the added feature that it can be changed to meet specific needs.

This solution has several basic flaws. If you are familiar with computer programming, you know that writing new software requires a large time commitment even for simple programs. The more complex the task, the longer it takes to complete. Unfortunately, teachers do not have the time to both write computer programs and teach. Even if they did, the amount of time and training required to learn programming would be prohibitive for most teachers.

As suggested earlier, programmers can be provided to actually write software as teachers request it. The problem is that most schools cannot afford to hire enough programmers to meet the daily requests of the teaching staff. Since programmers are expensive, it is doubtful that even the richest district could afford to hire a large enough programming staff to meet this need.

While on a limited basis providing programmers or programming skills to teachers can be helpful, it cannot provide the complete answer to an effective CAI system.

3. Authoring Systems

A third type of software is called an authoring system [2]. This system allows a teacher, naive in the area of computer programming, to put individualized lessons into the computer. A computer programmer develops software which guides the teacher through the creation of a computerized lesson. An authoring system is a tool used by the teacher to design and build educational lessons on the computer. This is done in much the same way as a teacher designs and builds other educational materials, such as dittos, transparencies, and diagrams for the classroom.

The advantage of this system is that it puts lesson development directly in the hands of the teacher, without the need for extensive training. Once the authoring system has been developed, the programmer is no longer needed, saving both programming salaries and lesson creation time. Since the teacher has complete control over the lesson creation process, lessons can be written that meet the specific needs of students, and modified as needed.

While an authoring system gives the teacher more flexibility than either canned software or locally developed software, it does have a price. The price a teacher must pay is in lesson development time. In either of the other two examples discussed, the teacher just uses existing software. With an authoring system, the teacher is actually responsible for writing the software. While this process is much easier and faster than programming, it still requires time on the teacher's part.

There are two ways to help alleviate this problem. The first is to collect all developed lessons into a library, which can be shared with all the teachers at a school. Given enough time, a large variety of lessons will be collected and will be available to all the teachers.

Second, teacher aides can be used to actually type lessons into the computer. The teacher's time is taken up only in the design of lessons on paper (filling out a lesson form), not the time typing on the keyboard. This further reduces the amount of teacher time needed to develop educationally sound computer assisted instruction.

While each of the software types discussed has its advantages and disadvantages in Computer Assisted Instruction, an authoring system provides the most versatility. It provides the teacher with flexibility at a low price. It puts lesson development under the control of the teacher and allows for the development of software to meet the individual needs of each student.

Good educational software is hard to find. Because of this, software becomes the deciding factor in choosing computer equipment. Equipment flexibility, reliability, and cost are all important factors in the selection process, but without flexible, well-designed educational software, a computer in the classroom is severely limited in its potential.

NOTES

1. PILOT is a language developed for computer assisted instruction. Several different versions are now available for the microcomputer. The most versatile PILOT development system the author has seen is Apple PILOT by the Apple Computer Company. It gives the programmer control of sound, graphics, text and question and answer sequences.

2. The San Juan Unified School District along with the California School for the Deaf received grants to develop a graphic CAI Authoring System. This system was programmed by Computer Advanced Ideas of Berkeley, California. The Authoring System is now being disseminated by the San Juan School District.

Blocks Authoring Language:
A Graphic CAI Authoring System

Ted Perry

San Juan Unified School District
6141 Sutter Avenue
Carmichael, California 95608
Tel. 916-944-3650

Developing a computer assisted instruction program seems like an exciting idea until one understands the complexity of the project. Buying good educational software seems like a good idea until one looks at the dearth of programs. Because of the lack of educational software and the complexity of the task of programming, most educators are not involved in Computer Assisted Instruction.

The Author language was developed to help fill the gap between the available and the desired programs. It was built for the teacher who has little or no programming experience.

The authoring system necessitates no programming expertise on the part of the teacher and literally walks the authoring teacher a step at a time through building a student curriculum. The system also makes full use of the graphic capabilities of the Apple computer.

The Author language has been piloted in more than 35 school districts and colleges with extremely favorable results. Students respond to the graphic capabilities of the system while teachers enjoy the ease of use and the automatic data collection program. The Author language system consists of several programs:

Teacher Authoring Program
- Allows the teacher to make use of the graphics library and combine graphic images with text for presentation to the student. The teacher also inputs the correct and incorrect answers and feedback appropriate to each response. This program is utilized only when writing a lesson.

Student Presentation Program
- Presents the lesson to the student and allows a student to interact with the previously authored program. It

asks the questions and gives the appropriate feedback for each response.

Graphics Development Program

- Develops graphic images for the graphics library. It enables the author to quickly create new images, utilize portions of old images or combine images. It can quickly fill an irregular shape with color and gives the author billions of colors and patterns to choose from.

Graphics Library Program

- A resource which is used when authoring a program. The teacher requests images from the graphics library and puts them into the lesson that is being written.

Data Management Program

- Keeps track of student progress and is actually a computerized lesson planner which enables the teacher to set up a sequence of lessons that matches the individual needs of each student.

It is difficult to decide where to start in describing this multi-faceted author language. Which comes first is hard to determine. Perhaps the best is to invite you to look through my eyes as I write a single computer assisted instruction lesson.

After the authoring diskette is put into drive one and a graphics library diskette is put in drive two, the authoring program is started. The computer then asks me if I wish to work on an old lesson or add a new lesson. In this demonstration, I would like to create a lesson from scratch so I respond: 'ADD A NEW LESSON.'

Next I am asked which area of the screen should contain text and which should contain graphics. I choose to make the lower 2/3 of the screen the text and to make the upper 1/3 graphics.

After pressing the ESC (escape) key to go on to the next sequence on the computer, I am presented with a blank screen and the word IMAGE at the bottom. The computer is asking me what graphic image I want. I can choose pictures from the graphic library to use in the lesson as I am building it. After typing the word TREE (which I know is on the graphics diskette), the computer responds by displaying the colored image of the tree on the screen and I manipulate its position utilizing the paddles. I repeat this sequence for two more trees, a witch, and a house. The upper 1/3 of my screen is filled with graphic images and I decide to escape from this part of the process.

The computer then asks me LABEL? and gives me an opportunity to place labels on or near the images. I choose to label the trees and the house.

When I finish with labels, the computer displays a sign across the screen which says, SAVING GRAPHICS PORTION. The intermediate results of my lesson are being saved. After the diskette stops, the computer prints TEXTUAL PORTION, asking me for text, questions, answers and feedback. For this demonstration, I typed the following:

```
+------------------------------------------+
|                                          |
|  TEXT:        There are  several  trees  |
|               on the screen.  How many   |
|               do you see?                |
|                                          |
|  RIGHT                                   |
|  ANSWER:      3  or three                |
|                                          |
|  FEEDBACK:    It sure is  hard to fool   |
|               you!!                      |
|                                          |
+------------------------------------------+
```

NOTE: The computer will accept either the digit 3 or the word three as the correct answer.

Next the computer asks me for expected wrong answers. I respond with other expected wrong answers and give feedback.

```
+---------------------------------------+
|                                       |
|  WRONG                                |
|  ANSWER:   1 OR 2                     |
|                                       |
|  FEEDBACK: Yes, you are right but I   |
|            think there are even       |
|            more trees on the          |
|            screen. Please try         |
|            again.                     |
|                                       |
+---------------------------------------+
```

The computer asks for more wrong answers and I press SPACE and ESCAPE. To state anything else will be considered a wrong answer. Then I give it FEEDBACK.

```
+---------------------------------------+
|                                       |
|  WRONG ANSWER: SPACE   and   ESCAPE   |
|                (the empty set)        |
|                                       |
|  FEEDBACK:     No, that is not cor-   |
|                rect. Please try       |
|                again.                 |
|                                       |
+---------------------------------------+
```

Having finished with question one, the computer now gives me several choices. I may use the same graphics and add more text and questions, or I may change the graphics as I add additional materials, or I may quit.

At this point I choose to end my low-level development task and as I tell the computer I have finished, it saves the text questions to the diskette, asks me to give the lesson a name and category, and to define the approximate grade level of usage. It also asks me to fill in author, date of development, and school of origin. Upon completion of those tasks, I am asked for a 70-character description of the lesson. We have termed this short description a one-line zinger! i.e., given several objects, the student will respond with the appropriate number in each subgroup.

Having completed authoring a one-question lesson, I proudly press RETURN and watch the computer combine the text and graphic information onto a diskette in a format to be presented to the student.

As the computer tells me it is compiling my lesson into that format, I sit and think about the other questions and changes I would like to make. I could put in some additional questions using these same graphics or I could change the graphics and put in a new question.

Because this is just a demonstration, I think I will leave the question as is. In any case, the computer has finished compiling my lesson and is asking me what I wish to do.

Unable to contain myself, I must run the student diskette to see my masterpiece in action!

The computer presents me with the graphic images across the top of my screen and asks me the appropriate questions.

Pleased with the performance of the computer but not with the quality of my curriculum, I turn off the computer and begin thinking about revising the presentation.

This presentation is meant to be an introduction to the workings of our multifaceted author language. It touched upon only a small portion of its capabilities. The school district is beginning the process of dissemination, with the proceeds going to help support the CAI program for the deaf. For further information, please contact Ted Perry at the San Juan Unified School District.

COMPUTER:

trees

house

Some of these things are trees. How many trees do you see?

MY RESPONSE: 3

COMPUTER
FEEDBACK: It sure is hard to fool you!!

COMPUTER:

Some of the things on the screen are trees. How many trees do you see?

MY RESPONSE:

7

COMPUTER FEEDBACK:

No, that is not correct. Please try again.

Project MASS: Microcomputer Assistance for Special Students

Margie Mason
Howard Smith
Kim Traub

Charleston Community Unit School District No. 1
410 West Polk Street
Charleston, Illinois 61920
Tel 217-345-2106

Project MASS (Microcomputer Assistance for Special Students) proposes to increase the effectiveness of the integration of handicapped students into the least restrictive environment mandated by PL 94-142 by using computer assisted instruction (CAI) to better prepare the students to function in the regular classroom and as a focal point for increasing communication between the regular classroom teachers and the special education staff.

PROJECT OBJECTIVES

Project MASS is a Title IV-C, ESEA, funded research-based project. We are using Apple microcomputers with 100 Learning Disabled (LD) and 55 Educable Mentally Handicapped (EMH) students who are enrolled in kindergarten through twelfth grade in the Charleston school system. We have a similar number of Special Education students not being exposed to CAI in two other districts who are serving for control groups. As a Title IV, ESEA, Part C project, the objectives for our first year are:

1) After Project MASS intervention, and by June 1, 1981, the target handicapped students' skill levels in mathematics and language skills will have increased at a .05 level of significance as compared to those of the control group handicapped students. This change will be measured by comparing results of the following tests: Iowa Test of Basic Skills (ITBS), Peabody Individualized Achievement Test (PIAT), Wide Range Achievement Test (WRAT), and a Basic Facts Test administered during October, 1980, and again during April/May, 1981.

2) After ten months of participation in the project, the regular classroom teachers will demonstrate gains in positive attitudes toward handicapped children and having them mainstreamed into their own classrooms at the .05 level of

significance as compared to those of control teachers as measured by the Rucker-Gable Education Programming Scale.

3) Compared to control group students, as measured by goal attainment scaling based on each student's Indivualized Education Plan (IEP) conducted as a limited pilot probe for both target and control groups in February, March and May of the project year, the target handicapped students will demonstrate increased progress in program goal attainment at the .05 level of significance.

TEACHER INSERVICE

The actual program involves nine Special Education and eighteen regular classroom teachers in Charleston. In order to prepare these teachers to participate, sixteen hours of inservice was offered to the Special Education teachers and eight hours of inservice to the regular classroom teachers during the summer of 1980. During one week of the summer workshops, all Project MASS teachers (regular and Special Education) received inservice training in methods of utilizing microcomputers to supplement regular instruction. After completing a unit on the elements of Instructional Design, the teachers, who had been grouped into teams consisting of one Special Education and two regular classroom teachers into whose classrooms students were being mainstreamed, evaluated existing software. Besides fostering a spirit of cooperation, this experience allowed the teachers to review a selection of software for their possible use, become critical consumers of existing software, and determine areas in which programs are needed. The teams are conferring on each Project MASS student's progress on a regular basis throughout the school year and select, design, or adapt computer programs to fit the student's evolving needs. The Special Education teachers learned enough programming in BASIC during a second week of summer workshops to ena-

ble them to tailor existing programs with merit to the particular needs of individual students and, in some cases, to write their own original programs. The project coordinators support these efforts and also write original software where needed. The Special Educators then incorporate the microcomputer programs into their lessons to provide drill and practice, and concept and skill development activities. Additional one and one-half hour workshops are offered on a monthly basis throughout the school year.

STUDENT PARTICIPATION

The handicapped students participate in Project MASS work on the microcomputer for a minimum of three 15-minute or two 20-minute sessions per week within the framework of their usual Special Education classes. No additional time is spent with the Special Education teacher other than what would normally be a part of the students' day. With its branching, color, sound, graphics and animation capabilities, the microcomputer provides drill and practice, and concept and skill development activities to raise the proficiency level of the handicapped student in his/her daily classwork and to develop skills which are lacking or deficient due to handicap. Some programs are used for positive reinforcement in behavior modification programs.

SOME SAMPLE SOFTWARE

Project MASS has both adapted existing software to meet the special needs of our population and developed new software in areas where we found no suitable programs. Examples of existing software which has been incorporated into our project include:

Hurkle
- an educational game from the Minnesota Educational Computing Consortium (MECC) in which the student locates a "hurkle" hiding on a horizontal line,

vertical line, 10 x 10 grid, or -5 x +5 grid. The students are given clues such as "GO NORTH" or "GO SOUTHEAST" after each guess of the location. We have adapted this for non-reading EMH students by adding arrows and changing the vocabulary to right-left.

Shell Games

- A program from Apple Computer, Inc. which provides a "shell" for true-false, multiple choice, or match column drills with the teacher's original questions. One version, which was used to prepare our high school EMH students for the U.S. Constitution test required for graduation, helped all these students pass this test on their first attempt, an almost unheard-of achievement.

Stay Afloat

- An educational game similar to Hangman which helps students with spelling and word patterns.

ABCD Order

- A drill on alphabetizing to the first, second or third letter.

Alphabet

- A program to teach the alphabet and keyboard for very young students.

Apple Bee

- A spelling program in which the student is shown a word and then must spell it. The teacher controls the words used, the length of display, the number of chances the student has to spell it correctly, and other variables in the program.

Addition

- A program designed to teach two-digit addition with and without regrouping to LD students by using color coding.

Capitals

- A program designed to teach and then drill on the rules of capitalization.

All software used in the project is documented as to subject, grade level. objectives, background information, and information to enable the teachers to modify the programs to their needs.

For further information on the project, please contact:

Ms. Margie Mason, Coordinator
Project MASS
Community Unit School District No. 1
410 W. Polk
Charleston, IL 61920

Microcomputer Selection
Process Model

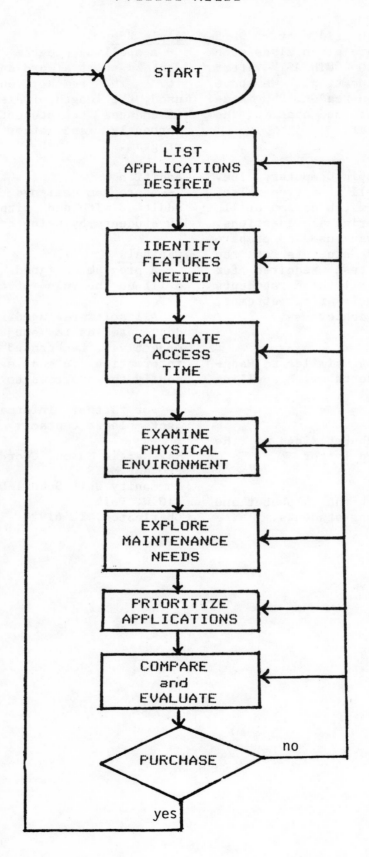

How to Select a Microcomputer System Using a Process Model

Pierre P. Barrette

Department of Curriculum, Instruction and Media
College of Education
Southern Illinois University at Carbondale
Tel 618-453-5764

In this presentation we examine a process model of selecting one or more microcomputer systems[1,2]. We also examine selected features common to many different microcomputers and attempt to relate these features to some uses teachers and students at any grade level or in any subject areas may have.

It must be stated categorically at the outset that no empirical research evidence exists to suggest that microcomputer brand "A" is "better" than microcomputer brand "B". It is agreed, however, that certain individuals and groups will favor one machine over another for different individual or collective reasons. There are many good microcomputers currently available and the new ones coming are even better.

The process of selecting a microcomputer is not as difficult as one would imagine. One must learn new terms and concepts in order to be able to make intelligent comparative assessments. The easy part, however, is to ultimately compare and make a choice of a particular machine. The most difficult part comes earlier. This part is associated with answering a number of questions about how it is planned to use a particular machine in the teaching/learning process. The more time spent on addressing the question of how it is planned to use the machine, the easier the ultimate purchase decision will be.

It should be remembered that there is no "final" choice in terms of microcomputers or microcomputer systems. The machines currently available will become outdated and obsolete a lot faster than many people realize. New models will be introduced. One should expect the new models to possess features not commonly available today. These new and enhanced features will be offered at pricing levels at or below the ones that currently exist.

There are many different ways to go about the process of selecting a microcomputer system. One should expect to receive all types of information from various people, including colleagues, hardware vendors and software vendors. Everyone, it appears, has a set of personal reasons why one should buy a particular brand or model. Information one receives can, and in some cases is likely to be, conflicting or completely erroneous. Be prepared to receive rumors about the weaknesses of one brand as opposed to the strengths of another. The virtue of objectivity has not become enhanced with the advent of microcomputers. In spite of this, one can proceed to make informed decisions about microcomputers by using a process model involving as few as seven major steps.

The first step in the process of selecting a microcomputer, or microcomputer system, is to create a written list of potential applications. This written list contains a series of statements about how it is planned to use the machine system. A list of such applications should include:

1. All planned uses which may involve students as they employ drill and practice, tutorial, simulation, instructional games, or other types of previously prepared program materials on a one-to-one basis.

2. All planned uses that may involve students on a one-to-one basis as they are involved in using microcomputers to acquire language or computer process skills using one or more of a number of high or low level languages.

3. All planned uses that may involve students utilizing microcomputers for monitoring, recording and analyzing real time events. These real time events are normally associated with conducting experiments in which analog to digital conversions are made by the microcomputer.

4. All planned uses by the teacher in which a microcomputer may be used for classroom demonstrations of any kind, as opposed to single one-to-one student use.

5. All planned uses by the teacher in which a microcomputer system may be used to facilitate the analysis and assessment of student progress.

6. Other uses for locally producing materials, instructional management, or other applications not previously described.

Literally thousands of specific microcomputer based applications have been developed and more will be developed. Your initial list is likely not to reflect all the applications that are possible, as you will discover new ones as time goes on. The important first step, however, is to write down each application separately. This is done readily using small cards.

Using small cards with headings printed on them is a great time saver, as well as being very helpful in making the ultimate choice(s). Use a separate card for each application you think you may make.

After writing down a specific application, you should then ask yourself what microcomputer system features may be needed for this application to be realized. An examination of a number of microcomputer features follows, together with a table of those features found in selected microcomputers.

When you have written down the application and the features needed for it, examine the question of access time very carefully. Access time is the actual amount of either one-to-one student contact time with a microcomputer or the contact time needed by the teacher for direct instructional presentations, or other teacher use. Access time, unfortunately, has seldom been considered in the selection process. It is likely to

SAMPLE APPLICATION CARDS

```
MICROCOMPUTER APPLICATION                  PRIORITY #

Assignment exercise
  Comparison of Pascal WHILE-DO
  vs. BASIC FOR-NEXT commands for 20 students.

  Estimated 2 hours key in and run time each.

----------------------------------------------------------------

FEATURES NEEDED                 ACCESS TIME _____ 40 hours/wk

- 48 K RAM
- monitor, B & W
- 2 floppy disk drives
- language card Pascal & BASIC
- printer for HC output



ENVIRONMENT:  Classroom & Media Center
```

```
MICROCOMPUTER APPLICATION                  PRIORITY #


Computer control process skill curriculum introduction.
Six students.  Grade 5
For 36 weeks at 2 hour/week/student




----------------------------------------------------------------

FEATURES NEEDED                 ACCESS TIME

- 48 K RAM                      One to One
- B & W MONITOR                 12 hours/week
- 2 FLOPPY DISK DRIVES
- LOGO LANGUAGE CARD OR ROM/pack



ENVIRONMENT: Math Lab
```

be one of the most important factors that will determine the success or failure of implementing a microcomputer based project. One may be able to double or even triple access time per dollar by knowing clearly the features needed for planned applications, and purchasing a different brand of microcomputer or microcomputer system to accommodate these needs. While there are certain advantages as well as disadvantages in having all microcomputers in a school the same brand, one should keep in mind that microcomputers are only tools, and one should select the best tools to get the job done--even though they may not have the same brand name.

The fourth step in the selection process is to examine all the physical environments where the microcomputer will be used for these applications. Without question, a great many applications will take place in the classroom. Special rooms can be set up for multiple microcomputer systems, but this may pose additional staffing questions as well as the possibility of problems in student control and scheduling. Aside from the classroom, one of the best locations for multiple microcomputer systems is the media center. In fact, the media center is rapidly becoming the logical choice in many schools, in order to provide additional student access time. Reserve and circulation of materials can be arranged with the media specialist. If there are a limited number of microcomputer systems, and access time is anticipated to be restricted, you should consider the need for student sign-up schedules.

Other physical environment considerations include sufficient grounded electrical power. Damage to microcomputers can occur if the power surges or drops because of other heavy power equipment. More important, however, is the possibility that with power surges or drops the programs that are running may crash. Be sure that the microcomputers are not on the same electrical circuit as that used for televised instruction.

Microcomputer generated interference can affect the quality of signals received on television sets near them. Static discharge from users crossing carpeted surfaces (especially in heated or low-humidity conditions) can easily cause programs being prepared or in use to crash. This is very frustrating to anyone who has been working extensively on a particular application and has not yet saved a version of it.

The physical environment where microcomputer systems are located will require supervision. Organization, care and control of materials for students will become increasingly important as the number of applications and the number of microcomputer systems increase. Plans should be made in anticipation of problems that will occur.

The fifth step in the selection process is associated with the issue of how maintenance service for microcomputer systems is to be provided. Ninety days is approximately the length of most warranties on microcomputers and system peripherals. You can anticipate a minimum average of five percent system failure time for each piece of equipment per year. As you list and examine the features needed, ask yourself, "Who is going to perform the periodic maintenance on the equipment?" and "Who is responsible for repairing the equipment when it breaks down?" Larger school districts have centralized media equipment repair programs. Many of these programs are now in the process of being upgraded to handle repair of solid state electronic machines. Check with them for any information they may have about the features or the equipment you plan on purchasing. If they do not have information about the equipment and you intend to acquire it anyway, it would be very wise to explore the maintenance issue with them further.

If your school district does not provide for central media equipment maintenance you will need to obtain maintenance from outside sources. One should estimate the annual maintenance cost to be approximately 10% of the capital cost of the equipment. This may or may not include the cost to upgrade the microcomputer system as manufacturers come out with new enhancements. One should not expect an over-friendly reception when looking for outside maintenance from a vendor near you who, for the sake of a few dollars, did not receive the bid for equipment.

Service contracts are available for most microcomputer system equipment. Generally, a service contract costs annually about 10% of the retail cost of the equipment. Service contracts vary widely and should be carefully examined to find out what they do or do not contain. Failure to anticipate service maintenance needs associated with microcomputers can seriously affect the implementation of a program, no matter how fine the statement of each of the applications.

Step six in the selection process is to sort the applications you plan and prioritize them. Sort on the basis of what you consider to be the most important applications that can realistically be accomplished, considering the access time available. This step occurs almost naturally as the list of desired applications continues to grow. Do not overstate to others what you can reasonably accomplish with the anticipated equipment and the time needed to integrate the planned applications into the curriculum. It takes time--a lot of time--to implement a project, even with one or two microcomputers. Save or use the additional applications not in the top priority to build a case for additional systems.

The final step is to compare the features available on various brands of microcomputers with those required for your applications. When doing the actual comparisons, be sure to inquire from vendors if this is the latest version of a particular model you may be considering. Compare several brands. If possible, ask individuals who own a particular piece of equipment what their experiences have been with it and with any service problems. Remember to focus on the features you desire for yourself and your students. Once the decision has been made, consider the possibility of group or network purchasing and how this relates to providing service.

The following is a list and brief description with comments associated with selected microcomputer features that one may want to consider. Comparative justice to each item on the list would literally require at least one or more complete books. It should be understood that any statements made about microcomputer features or microcomputer systems in this presentation are absolutely dependent upon what is available today and not what may become available.

MICROPROCESSOR

The heart of any microcomputer is its microprocessor. For most educational applications that rely on the use of a microcomputer to deliver instruction by running prepared or purchased programs, the question of which microprocessor one should have is usually not important. This of course does not hold true if the microprocessor is itself the object of instruction within one of these programs. Over one hundred and thirty different microprocessors have been fabricated to date. The most common ones have been 8-bit devices and over half of current microcomputers use 8-bit microprocessors. Sixteen-bit microprocessors will become more popular in the educational market in the next few years for a number of very practical reasons, including higher graphic capabilities and greater addressable memory. Unless one has specific applications that require a particular 8- or 16-bit microprocessor, such as studying the architecture and instruction set of the processor, one need not be much concerned whether the

MICROCOMPUTER FEATURES TABLE

MODEL	Source	Suggested list	Microprocessor	Bit size	Color capable	User available RAM	Number of keys	Available ROM	ROM/RAM Cartridge	Cassette Included	Floppy Disk
MODEL "R"	a	249.00	8080A	8	Y	16K	53	2K	N	Y	NA
VIC 20	b	299.95	6502A	8	Y	3.5K	66	16K	Y	*	*
TRS-80 Color	c	399.95	6809A	8	Y	4K	53	8K	Y	*	*
Challenger C1-P	d	479.00	6502	8	N	4K	53	10K	N	Y	*
TI 99/4A	e	595.00	9900	16	Y	16K	53	26K	Y	*	*
Atari 400	f	630.00	6502	8	Y	8K	57	10K	Y	*	*
TRS 80 Model III	c	699.00	Z80	8	N	4K	65	4K	N	*	*
Commodore 2001	b	795.00	6502	8	N	8K	64	14K	N	*	*
Challenger C4-P	d	879.00	6502C	8	Y	8K	53	10K	Y	*	*
Challenger C8-P	d	895.00	6502A	8	Y	8K	63	10K	Y	*	*
Atari 800	f	1080.00	6502	8	Y	16K	57	10K	Y	*	*
Excidy Sorcerer	g	1295.00	Z80	8	N	16K	63	4K	N	*	*
Heath 88	h	1295.00	Z80	8	N	16K	72	8K	N	*	*
Apple II+	i	1330.00	6502	8	Y	16K	52	8K	Y	*	*
Bell & Howell	j	1420.00	6502	8	Y	16K	52	8K	Y	*	*
IBM Personal	k	1595.00	8088	16	Y	16K	83	40K	N	*	*
Commodore 8032	b	1795.00	6502	8	N	16K	73	14K	N	*	*
Osborne 1	l	1795.00	8080A	8	N	60K	68	4K	N	*	*
Compucolor II-3	m	1895.00	8080A	8	Y	8K	--	16K	N	*	2
Heath H-8	h	1970.00	8080A	8	N	16K	73	1K	N	*	*

* Optional. Note: Prices are manufacturers suggested retail prices.
Actual prices vary extensively depending upon quantity and special promotions.

resident processor is an 8- or 16-bit slice machine.

It should be noted that most microcomputer manufacturers do not make their own microprocessors. They purchase them from original equipment manufacturers and assemble them with other parts into a microcomputer.

COLOR

Whether color is an important feature to have or not is often a judgment based upon an individual's preference. It is akin to asking whether a color or black-and-white TV is needed. At this time little or no empirical research evidence exists to suggest that color produces significant learning changes for students involved with microcomputer based programs. Of course, if color is the object of a program, then the argument does not hold. If past research involving use of color in film, television, slides, etc., can be an indicator, it is likely that color associated with microcomputers will yield similar findings. It may not make much sense, however, to insist on color as a feature, go out and purchase or lease a number of commercial or proprietary color-based programs, and then equip the microcomputer with a black-and-white monitor to "save" money. One can purchase a very fine microcomputer and black-and-white monitor for less than the cost of a color monitor itself. One can also purchase a very fine microcomputer capable of generating color and not use the color feature at all, since other features in the same equipment may be more important.

USER AVAILABLE RAM

This feature relates to the actual amount of user available read/write memory a microcomputer has. This is an important feature to consider. The emphasis is upon the term "user available" as opposed to the stated amount of actual read/write random access memory that is often present. The features table states the amount of user available RAM. Random access read/write memory (RAM) of a microcomputer is located in one or more small chips within it. Programs and data can be stored, retrieved and erased from these chips. The electronic size of a random access read/write memory is currently measured in K byte units [3]. The abbreviation K (standing for Kilo) is used as a convenient method of expressing slightly over one thousand bytes of storage [4]. A microcomputer with an 8-bit microprocessor can be equipped in various sizes of addressable read/write memory (RAM) ranging up to 64K. It must be noted that by employing special bank select chips inside a microcomputer the read/write memory can be extended beyond this stated limit. The initial price of a microcomputer normally reflects a much smaller read/write RAM. Extra memory costs are additional. One must purchase additional read/write RAM chips or plug-in read/write RAM packs to increase the size of the memory for many applications. The actual amount of "user available" read/write memory in K units is often considerably less than what the machine actually possesses. This is because, for many machines, part of the read/write RAM memory is used to store special computer programs that make the microcomputer operate. Such programs may include high level language interpreters, compilers, communication programs, and very often part or all of the disk operating system of a particular microcomputer.

When examining the "user available" RAM features ask the question, "How much user available read/write RAM memory will I need?" If you don't know, then it may be wise to purchase as much read/write RAM as possible, even with the first microcomputer. Ask vendors how much user available read/write RAM is actually available, even though you may have purchased as much as is possible with a particular brand. As you compare various brands, pay particular attention to the amount of read/write RAM memory that must be occupied by different high level computer languages. Consider also the later comments associated with ROM/RAM cartridges when examining user available RAM.

KEYSET

The keyset of a microcomputer is one of its most important features. The term "keyboard" is often used instead of keyset. Very few microcomputers have precisely the same <u>set</u> of keys even though they may have a similar <u>number</u> of keys. Keys needed on a microcomputer depend very much on the applications one has in mind. The initial cost of a microcomputer normally provides little guidance of what the keys available with it do. There are many excellent microcomputers at the low cost end that have keysets superior to others at the higher cost end. Here are some questions one should ask:

1. Does the native keyset include all ASCII characters without any hardware modifications or software enhancements? You may need a full ASCII character set if you plan to involve yourself with local production of materials using lower case characters, square brackets, etc. Upper and lower case and full ASCII adapter chips can be purchased at additional cost for many microcomputers.

2. Does the native keyset include a numeric keypad? Applications with extensive amounts of numeric input may need this feature. With some systems it is included; with others, optional.

3. Does the native keyset provide user definable keys? User definable keys are special individual keys which permit one to define how they will operate when pressed. Normally, a user definable key can be programmed to generate a special character or represent a predefined procedure. One application for them may be the ability, in conjunction with other keys, to create outputted numeric or arithmetic subscripts and superscripts. Another may be the ability to define sigmas and limits associated with them. A third application may be associated with defining keys for hexadecimal entry. These and many other special uses may become valuable timesaving features, and may also extend the list of possible applications.

4. Does the native keyset also include graphic keys? This feature may be particularly important in order to prepare monitor graphic images from the keyboard. Many keysets place actual partial graphic symbols on their keys. Look closely at your applications to determine if the need to prepare graphic images is an important feature, and whether or not a particular brand of microcomputer has graphic keys as a standard offering.

5. How many of the non-control type of keys in the keyset are individually repeatable with a single key stroke?

6. Does the native keyset include clearly defined cursor control keys?

7. Can keys used to interrupt a program be disabled manually as well as under software control?

AVAILABLE ROM

ROM is the acronym for Read Only Memory. This is a special random access memory of a microcomputer. One can only read from this memory, and not write into it. The read only ROM is currently located on one or more chips in the microcomputer. Often it is the part where manufacturers place their high level computer language interpreter or other computer instructions needed for the machine to operate. The size of the read only memory (ROM) will vary from one manufacturer to another; it is also measured in K units, similar to RAM.

Information stored in ROM is permanently stored. It is not lost when the power is turned off as it is in read/write RAM. Some ROM chips can store complete computer application programs needed for instruction, management or communication. If possible, have the vendor explain what the various ROM chips do. Often read only memory chips, ROM, are conveniently housed in special plug-in removable containers called cartridges or command modules.

ROM/RAM CARTRIDGES

Some microcomputers have a feature which permits the user to plug in special cartridges that contain either additional read/write random access memory (RAM) or a special read only memory (ROM). ROM cartridges can contain any number of programs such as a different language, an instructional program, a management program, a communications program, etc. Any program stored on a floppy disk can be prepared for permanent storage into one or more ROM chips, and the chip(s) then loaded into a cartridge. Usually there is one program on each cartridge. An advantage of a ROM cartridge is that there are no moving parts and one may have rather large and sophisticated programs stored in it. A floppy disk or cassette storage device is not usually needed unless additional student performance monitoring information or other data incidental to the program needs to be recorded for later use. ROM cartridges available for specific brands of microcomputers are not compatible with other brands or with each other.

CASSETTE DECKS

Cassette storage decks for microcomputers employ an actual or slightly modified audiotape recorder/player. There are special digital cassette decks, but these are not the type discussed here. Cassette decks are still a very popular feature with microcomputer users because of their low initial cost compared to floppy disk drives. Some brands of microcomputers include a cassette deck built into the microcomputer chassis as part of the basic system. Other manufacturers provide a receptacle in the chassis and sell the cassette deck separately or expect the user to provide the cassette recorder/player. The time needed to load or save a program or data to and from a cassette into the read/write memory of a microcomputer will vary from one machine to another. Examine closely the time needed for this process and compare the speeds on different cassette based microcomputers. Normally, programs and data cannot be loaded or saved as quickly as with a disk drive. However, initial costs and other considerations may compel one to elect the cassette deck for storage.

One may also want to consider another type of storage device called a stringy floppy. This employs a strip of magnetic tape in an endless loop cartridge similar in principle to an audio cartridge. It costs more than a cassette deck but considerably less than a floppy disk unit and has high K storage, very rapid load and save times, and has enjoyed a reputation for being very reliable.

FLOPPY DISK DRIVES

Floppy disk drives that use 5-1/4 inch diskettes are generally available only as optional features for most microcomputers. One of the microcomputer systems listed on the table includes two disk drives as part of the basic system. Floppy disk drives for different manufacturers are not compatible with each other, for a number of technical and planned reasons.

Floppy disks can store large amounts of information as measured in K units. One must be careful to ask the question, "How much user available space is there on the first, second or third diskette?" Many floppy disks contain a computer program called an operating system stored on the first diskette. This operating system may consume up to one-half or more of the maximum possible storage space on the first diskette, leaving little available to the user.

Floppy disk drives are classified as single density, double density, double sided, or double density-double sided. Single density disk drives permit 35 or more concentric tracks on one side of a diskette to be accessed so that programs or data can be stored or retrieved from various sections of the available tracks. A double density disk drive literally doubles the number of tracks or squeezes twice as much information into the existing tracks. Double sided means that both surfaces of the diskette are used.

The drives are electromechanical devices and as such are more susceptible to failure than ROM cartridges. The heads of the disk drive need to be cleaned; this should be part of the periodic maintenance provided through the school media program. Training of students in care and handling of diskettes will greatly assist in reducing disk drive failure due to damaged or contaminated floppy disks.

HARD DISK DRIVES

Hard disk drives using a 5-1/4 inch or larger sealed disk are becoming more popular as an optional feature. The advantage is one is able to store larger amounts of information, often measured in MB (megabytes). A typical single 5-1/4 inch hard disk drive system will cost four or more times a single floppy disk drive system but also can store ten or more times what a single floppy disk can store. Generally, the larger the size of the hard disk and the more tracks it has, the more it can store. Some single platter hard disk drives available for microcomputers have storage capacities in excess of 30 million bytes, 30 MB.

At the present time hard disk drives

are coming into more common use with microcomputers. Usually one must purchase the hard disk system from a different company, not the manufacturer of the microcomputer. This will change as more microcomputer manufacturers begin including hard disks in their line of equipment.

An important mechanical difference between a floppy and a hard disk system is the way the magnetic head works. With a floppy disk system the tiny magnetic read/write head makes physical contact onto the floppy disk surface. With a hard disk system the head literally floats above the disk surface. It never touches the disk. If it did, a phenomenon known as a "head crash" would occur. Head crashes can be caused by dust or other surface contaminants, by sudden jolts, or most often by power failures.

The actual physical environment where the hard disk system may be located should be carefully considered. The matter of preventing head crash should be thoroughly explored with vendors.

Finally, the extent to which a hard disk drive gives you a cost advantage may be somewhat less than you would expect by comparing the storage capacity of hard disk and floppy disk drives. You cannot duplicate the hard disk file in its entirety as you can a floppy disk. Backup files must be copied using other equipment which you may need to purchase.

HIGH LEVEL LANGUAGES

Microcomputer manufacturers normally supply at least a single dialect of BASIC as the high level language with each system they sell. Dialects among different manufacturers are not compatible, especially in the area of graphics. Most microcomputer manufacturers contract with an outside independent company to produce the language dialect for them. Such an outside company designs specific enhancements of a high level language which the microcomputer manufacturer hopes will sustain a competitive sales advantage. Other high level languages can be purchased from either the original manufacturer or some other vendor. These include Pascal, PILOT, LOGO, LISP, FORTRAN, FORTH, COBOL, APL, Smalltalk, and others. They can be purchased on cassette, disk, ROM cartridges or individual ROM's.

The UCSD Pascal language is becoming increasingly popular in secondary math and science because of its structured approach to learning how to program. The language is also particularly noteworthy as a high level language because its design permits it to be the most machine independent such language developed to date. Machine independent implies that programs created on one brand of microcomputer will also operate on other brands. This is particularly important when one takes into account the exchanging of application programs among microcomputer system users. One can expect computer languages of all types to evolve with enhanced features involving graphics, speech and image recognition in the next few years. One can expect these languages to be available on cassette, floppy disk or ROM packs.

OPERATING SYSTEMS

Operating systems are special computer programs that manage the storage and retrieval of other programs and of data from the read/write RAM or read only (ROM) memory of a microcomputer to a disk or other peripheral. A microcomputer manufacturer that offers disk storage devices as optional features will also provide at least one operating system. There are a great variety of operating systems with a wide range in quality available today, but most are not compatible with each other, with the exception of Pascal.

Any applications that require exten-sive storing and retrieving of information from disks become very dependent on the capabilities and limitations of the operating system. If you are not, or choose not to become, conversant with the features of various operating systems, it would be most appropriate to spend additional time speaking with different people to understand this most important feature. It may also be appropriate to examine how various operating systems provide or do not provide for security, to prevent unwarranted access to the disk based information files.

Operating systems are in a constant state of change. Examine closely with vendors the question of what the impact of a sudden "update" will be on application programs you have developed or purchased that are stored on disks. One might have to convert a few or perhaps hundreds or thousands of diskettes if there is a major change in the vendor supplied operating system. Another important question to raise is what hardware changes will be needed if the operating system is updated. While vendors cannot predict what will happen, they can tell you what has happened.

LOW LEVEL LANGUAGE

For some insructional applications the need for a low level language such as an assembler exists. This is particularly true when teaching assembly level programming. For the most part assemblers are not included in the vendor price, even though machine level access may be available. The architecture desired and instruction set available become important selection considerations, especially as they relate to how extensive and complete the available written documentation for the system is.

For other applications associated with modifying resident operating systems, compilers or interpreters, or including efficient machine level call procedures within a high level applications program, the need for access to a well documented low level language will likely exist. Vendors and manufacturers should be consulted directly for information. Critiques through many periodical articles help in this effort.

PRINTER

Few microcomputer manufacturers offer printers as part of their basic system. Printers are typically produced by other companies. Some microcomputer manufacturers, however, are beginning to offer the interfaces--i.e., the proper physical and electrical connections needed to link the microcomputer and the printer---as part of the basic cost. Be aware that the standard for these connections is in the process of being changed.

Printers are either impact or non-impact. The most common are the dot matrix impact printers. There are literally hundreds of different models of printers. In the minimum case, you may want a printer that will print all of the ASCII characters and graphic characters your microcomputer generates. One can and possibly should include, as a printer feature, the ability to provide a printout (black and white) of whatever is displayed on the monitor. There are several printers with outstanding features that have just recently become available at extremely reasonable cost. Check with several computer stores.

MONITORS

Examining the microcomputer features table one can quickly determine if a monitor is included in the purchase price. Monitors vary extensively in quality, especially for the low end cost black-and-white. Green phosphorus screens on monitors are desirable for those who make extensive use of the monitor for displaying text information or with certain high level languages.

One should carefully compare at least two different monitors using the same microcomputer and the same program before selecting a monitor. If one plans to employ an 80-column microcomputer display, it becomes critical that the monitor be able to operate in the frequency range of 12 MHz for high quality resolution of the character information that is displayed.

Some microcomputer manufacturers include or provide optional adapters to permit the use of a regular television receiver. These radio frequency (RF) adapters generally cannot provide as clear and distinct an image as those with a direct electrical video connection as is found in monitors.

TEXT CHARACTERS/LINES

Microcomputers have different capabilities to display text characters on monitors. One normally measures the number of characters that can fit onto a single horizontal line and then the number of possible lines that can be displayed on the screen. The table includes only the first level of text characters per line. Many microcomputers have the ability to display different numbers of characters per line and different numbers of lines. Examine what comes with the basic microcomputer. Check the readability of the displayed characters, especially if both upper and lower case with descenders are included. It should be noted that graphics programs are available as options so that various combinations of shapes of characters, number of text characters per line and number of lines can be changed.

GRAPHICS RESOLUTION

The ability of a microcomputer to faithfully reproduce an image is at this time somewhat limited. This limitation is due in part to whether the microcomputer uses an 8- or 16-bit microprocessor, the amount of read/write or special video RAM memory space available for graphics, the performance features of a device called the video ROM and the frequency response of the monitor. One can expect much higher quality graphic images to be generated with a 16-bit processor. Nevertheless, an 8-bit processor can generate graphic images, but of varying quality. Most microcomputers have the ability to generate one or more levels of graphic quality, besides the level used for text characters. Some microcomputer manufacturers have recently introduced new high level language commands that easily permit graphic animation.

Examine various microcomputer(s) you may be considering, together with the high level language you anticipate using, to see if you can mix both graphics and text information in the same area on the screen. Examine again the question of how much user available read/write RAM memory you will have actually available for the non-graphic parts of a program. If you anticipate graphics to be an important feature for locally produced programs, this will help in your choice of a microcomputer.

There are many other features of microcomputers that could be discussed and may be needed in the applications you define. These may include the presence of sound generated from a microcomputer, the availability of special slots or ports to plug in additional so-called peripheral cards or parts, the ability to interconnect microcomputers to form a local network, etc. If these and other features are desired, check their availability and cost from the vendors and manufacturers.

It is important to remember that microcomputers and microcomputer systems are in a rapid state of change. The many features that are optional today are likely to become standard in a few short years as newer fabrication technologies permit their inclusion with little or no additional cost. There are many good microcomputers in the market today and the ones coming are even better.

VENDORS

Manu-tronics, Inc.
9115 26th Avenue
Kenosha, WI 53140
  Tel 414-694-7700

Commodore Business Machines, Inc.
3330 Scott Boulevard
Santa Clara, CA 95051

Radio Shack
A Division of Tandy Corporation
One Tandy Center
Fort Worth, TX 76102

Atari Consumer Division
1265 Borregas Avenue
P. O. Box 427
Sunnyvale, CA 94086
  Tel 408-745-2038

Texas Instruments, Inc.
U. S. Consumer Products Group
2301 West University
Lubbock, TX 79048
  Tel 806-741-3737

Ohio Scientific, Inc.
1333 S. Chillicothe Road
Aurora, OH 44202
  Tel 216-562-5177

Exidy Systems, Inc.
1234 Elko Drive
Sunnyvale, CA 94086
  Tel 408-734-4831

Heath Company
Benton Harbor, MI 49022
  Tel 616-482-3200

Apple Computer, Inc.
102260 Bandley Drive
Cupertino, CA 95014
  Tel 408-496-1010

Bell & Howell
Audiovisual Products Division
7100 North McCormick Road
Chicago, IL 60645
  Tel 312-673-3300

NOTES

1. Microcomputer: As employed in this presentation, an FCC Class B
    computer. It employs a microprocessor and has memory. Most micro-
    computers also include a keyboard. Commonly known also as a person-
    al computer or desktop computer. Handheld computers are not the
    type under consideration.

2. Microcomputer system: The combination of a microcomputer together
    with peripherals such as visual display device (monitor), cassette
    deck, floppy disk, hard disk, game paddles, modem, graphics tablet,
    light pens, printer, etc.

3. A byte typically reflects a single character such as a letter, num-
    ber or other symbol. A byte associated with 8-bit microcomputers
    contains eight binary digits.

4. The unit K actually represents 1024 bytes and not 1000 bytes.

Index

BOOKS ON COMPUTERS AND EDUCATION

MICROCOMPUTERS IN K-12 EDUCATION
First Annual Conference Proceedings
Pierre Barrette, Editor

Many school districts are faced with the integration of microcomputers into their systems. Discussions on how to deal with the problems and changes caused by the use of computers in the school is the subject of this annual conference at Southern Illinois University. *1982. $30.00. 0-914894-32-3.*

"Microcomputers in K-12 Education *is extremely relevant, timely, and well organized. Each chapter provides the address and telephone number of the author(s), thereby enabling any questions to be answered directly. Strongly recommended as must reading for everyone in all levels of education that are now using or are considering using microcomputers for teaching or administration."* Choice.

MICROCOMPUTERS IN K-12 EDUCATION
Second Annual Conference Proceedings
Pierre Barrette, Editor

The second Annual Conference on Microcomputers in K-12 Education focuses on the expanding use of microcomputers in education and new developments in the field. The papers to be presented at the conference will be included in this forthcoming book. *1983. $30.00. 0-914894-87-0.*

Coming soon. . .

THE MICROCOMPUTER AND THE SCHOOL LIBRARY MEDIA SPECIALIST
Pierre Barrette

Expanding use of microcomputers and information handling systems has greatly improved the capabilities of the school media center. It has also created a need for more information by the media center specialist. This comprehensive new book explains the possibilities, capabilities, and uses of microelectronics, computers, and information science. It covers the history of microelectronics, explains keyboards, storage machines and media, how to organize and handle digital electronic media, the use of monitors, digital electronic communication, printers, peripherals, computer languages and programs, and operating systems. Media center specialists will also find helpful the chapters on instructional authoring systems, instructional programs and how to select them, management application programs, professional development, physical facilities required, card catalog conversion, and maintenance and repair of microcomputer systems and electronic equipment. Companion programs on diskettes will be offered separately. This book will be published in early 1984. *Price not yet set. 0-914894-93-5.*

OTHER BOOKS OF INTEREST AVAILABLE FROM COMPUTER SCIENCE PRESS

LEARNING BASIC STEP BY STEP

Student Book, $15.95, 0-914894-49-8
Teacher's Guide, $17.95, 0-914894-33-1
Examination Package, $30.00, 0-914894-89-7
Vern McDermott and Diana Fisher

Carefully designed to develop programming skills without frustration, this hardcover text offers thorough explanations, demonstration problems, and skill development exercises in each chapter. Machine specific for APPLE II, PET, TRS-80 Models I and III, ATARI 400/800, and HP-2000 computers. *1982.*

BITS 'n BYTES ABOUT COMPUTING
A Computer Literacy Primer
Rachelle Heller and Dianne Martin

Complete explanations, detailed educational objectives, and over 100 suggested activities help K-8 instructors teach their students about computers—how they work, what they do for us, and how they affect our lives. No computer science background necessary. *1982. $17.95. 0-914894-26-9.*

Highly recommended for junior high, senior high, and general audience. This spendid book is directed toward computer literacy training for elementary teachers. . .Chapters on the origin of computers, how they work, and what they do for us are particularly lucid, enlightening, and remarkably complete. Science Books and Films.

SIMPLE PASCAL
James J. McGregor and Alan H. Watt

This book offers simple, practical examples to help beginning programmers and students learn the Pascal programming language, and builds a solid foundation for further study of advanced programming techniques and computer science. *1982. $12.95. 0-914894-72-2.*

STRUCTURED BASIC AND BEYOND
Wayne Amsbury

This excellent book teaches not only the BASIC programming language, but also provides a firm foundation in good programming principles. An excellent choice for independent study or for a course text. *1980. $14.95 paper, 0-914894-16-1. $16.95 cloth, 0-914894-90-0.*

Highly recommended. Junior High, Senior High, General Audience and College levels. Science Books and Films.

ESSENTIALS OF COBOL PROGRAMMING:
A STRUCTURED APPROACH
Gerald N. Pitts and Barry L. Bateman

The COBOL language is thoroughly covered in this well-organized new book, providing students with an understanding of how the various aspects of COBOL are interrelated. Questions and indexes at the end of each chapter make this an excellent choice for a course text or for independent study. *1982. $14.95. 0-914894-34-X.*

PASCAL: AN INTRODUCTION TO METHODICAL PROGRAMMING Second Edition
William Findlay and David Watt

Programming principles, good style, and a methodical approach to program development are emphasized in this improved and expanded introduction to the Pascal programming language. *1982. $16.95. 0-914894-73-0.*

Highly recommended for senior high, college and general audience. This book has the virtue of being concise and clear. Meant to be an introductory text to PASCAL, it is on the one hand refreshingly simple and on the other surprisingly sophisticated. A novice programmer would have no trouble in understanding this book. An advanced programmer would also feel challenged. Science Books and Films.